THE
WINNER'S
NOTEBOOK

THE
WINNER'S
NOTEBOOK

Theodore Isaac Rubin, M.D.

TRIDENT PRESS  NEW YORK

Library of Congress Catalog Card Number: 67-23593

Published by Trident Press, a division of Simon & Schuster, Inc.,
630 Fifth Avenue, New York, N.Y. 10020

Printed in the United States of America

For my friends,
Henry Horowitz, M.D.
and
Joey Unger

This book would not have been possible without the very extensive training I received at the American Institute for Psychoanalysis. That training was largely inspired by the works of the late Dr. Karen Horney.

Though I never had the chance to meet Dr. Horney, I feel that I know her through her works and I shall always be grateful to her for them. I want to thank all my teachers at the Institute and particularly Dr. Nathan Freeman. Some few of us have the privilege of knowing a great and wise human being at some time in our lives. I have now known Nathan Freeman for a good many years.

CONTENTS

Contents

Contents

Contents

Introduction

Are you a winner or a loser?

A winner is a person who relates successfully to himself and to other people. A loser does not! Relating successfully to ourselves and to other people means a richer, more rewarding and happier life in all areas of human existence and endeavor.

Here and there I shall refer to "Max." Max will at times be a boy friend or girl friend, wife or husband, boss, colleague, client, audience or anybody else with whom you have or desire to have a relationship.

This is not a theoretical book, nor is it a psychiatric text. It isn't a substitute for psychiatric treatment, and it certainly is not a guide to do-it-yourself psychoanalysis. Indeed, this book could have as correctly been called "The Winner's Workbook." This is so because, as in psychoanalytic treatment, where the patient as well as the doctor does much of the "work," here, too, *you* must work. There are no pat formulas here, no quick pills for success. We will open up new doors and get rid of many old, destructive and paralyzing skeletons and ghosts. However, you must share in the work. This may not be easy, but please remember that our endeavor is completely in the service of constructive, successful living.

Real understanding of your self and Max will make you a happier, healthier human being.

"If I am not for myself who will be? If I am only for myself what am I? If not now, when?"

—from the *Talmud*

SECTION I

Assets

This first section deals with human assets. Many people don't know that they have them. Many people don't know what human assets are. How about you? I think of these assets as seeds of health. I do so because they offer the possibility of germination, growth and change.

You surely have many assets, but do you recognize them for what they are? Perhaps you haven't realized that they are assets. I am going to discuss a number of important ones in this section. Some of them will overlap. This is largely so because they are interrelated and almost never exist in isolation. None of us has all of them, but all of us have some.

Having them, however, is not enough. Getting acquainted with them is not enough. *Owning* them is the thing; owning them so that you know that they are assets, so that you know how much health and growth and good relating with Max can come from them. But this is still not enough. Owning them means that you do not take your assets for granted and that you never minimize them. It is vital that you appreciate their great value and it is crucial that you know that they are yours, to be used in your behalf and to be used in relating to Max. Owning them in the fullest sense is extremely important in raising and maintaining your self-esteem, and self-esteem is an absolute essential in being a winner. But more about self-esteem later.

Read this next section carefully and then reread it—study it—digest it—because I want you to enjoy what you've got, secure in the knowledge that what you've got is really *yours*.

The insistent fact of life itself

Of course, you are alive. But don't let's joke this one away. Are you convinced that being alive at any age makes change and growth possible? I have seen patients who have been chronically ill and confined in state hospitals for over forty years get well enough to leave and then go on to lead useful lives. This has happened spontaneously, often without any "logical" explanation whatsoever. Yes, protoplasm—living matter—has an inherent way of bouncing back, of responding, of resisting obliteration. So to be alive is to have hope, and hope is no small item. People can grow and become healthier as long as they live, whatever their age.

How wonderful—you are here, now. You are breathing, hearing, feeling and seeing. You are alive and *growing*.

A long-living healthy family

You were very wise to have chosen parents who are living long and healthy lives. Most physicians agree that much of the stuff that accounts for long life and health is inherited. This includes arteries that age slowly and an efficient disease-resistant system. But even if your parents were a poor choice in this area, there is still much hope. You may have inherited better possibilities through genes donated by other ancestors. Also—

4

medicine has made and continues to make considerable progress to help keep us alive longer and longer with each succeeding generation.

A *history of personal good health*

How fortunate, if you have not had a serious illness, major surgery, or a crippling disease. In addition to the obvious physical benefits of having a healthy, well-developed body, there are some very important emotional ones. An individual blessed with good health from very early life has a healthy physical image of himself which contributes considerably to his self-acceptance and self-esteem. In short, he feels good about himself as a physical entity. He likes the feel of himself physically and this is converted in part to a good emotional feeling about himself. This also contributes to a sense of physical sureness and confidence, making it easier to deal with other people on a healthy level.

If you have a good physical history, there is a better chance that you are more capable of physical enjoyment. You have a good feeling about your body and haven't repressed much of your feeling for it. You will have less of a tendency to separate your intellect from your body in an attempt to live mainly on an intellectual level. There will be more of a chance for a healthy body-mind integration rather than a destructive dichotomy. In your psychic structure—your concept of yourself—you will not have lost touch with a most important part of you—your body. You are ahead because there is a large part of you that you like and accept, and this contributes a great deal to your self-esteem.

A home—with parents

No institution, however efficient, can substitute adequately for the close personal and emotional investment of parents. Living with parents who *care* offers the opportunity for identification—a feeling for who you are as a human being, sexually and otherwise (more about this later)—as well as the establishment of values. Whatever else your parents may have been to you (good or bad) they have given you in some part a sense of right and wrong and a sense of who you are and what is what in this world. They have also provided you with a sense of family and ethnic identification, which contributes a great deal to a feeling of belonging. Hopefully, they have provided much more. Suffice it to say here that institutions often do remarkable work, but at best they are poor substitutes for family and parents. So, if you were brought up as part of a regular family group, with a mother and a father, you are well ahead of the game.

Having brothers and sisters

Being one of several children in a family has given you a further sense of belonging, in this case being a member of a team. Knowing that one is part of a family and has brothers and sisters who care and have common responsibilities, in which the good of all is concerned, adds considerably to early security. This also provides an opportunity for early experience in relating to other people in close harmony. This experience will be paralelled again and again in the future—in (healthy) rivalries, teamwork, etc., and you will have had an early head start.

Responsible parents

To have had parents who were fairly well adjusted, living together, with no history of antisocial behavior and who made a fair community adjustment is no small asset. Parents who have been a fairly normal part of the community structure have given you a good bridge to the outside world. This gives you a sense of orientation to your environment and a feeling of belonging, as well as a first step in feeling who you are in this world.

A mother and father capable of mutual understanding

Have your parents shared common interests and were they compatible with each other to the extent that they could work out differences and keep the lines of communication open within the family unit?

Then these were people who could talk. They didn't sulk; have huge temper tantrums; sabotage each other in blatant or subtle vindictive enterprises; abandon each other periodically; make inordinate demands on each

7

other to demonstrate devotion and fidelity; maintain a tight, controlled armed truce; sound off mutual complaints to friends, neighbors and children; have drinking bouts or long depressions or long periods of separate sleeping, etc. Your parents never exploited you in fighting each other, nor did they make you their mediator or judge. Yes, these were people who could have differences, who could get angry and who could communicate adequately to resolve their differences, because they were mature enough and also had enough in common to ultimately provide grounds for mutual understanding. These parents have, by example, provided you with both know-how and hope, in communicating with your fellowmen. They have in effect "told" you, deep down where it counts, that people can reach each other and that the world is not a jungle. This, in itself, can contribute much to your basic security and to your confidence in relating to Max.

Parents who love each other

By love, I mean that they had sufficient self (more about self later) to care about each other more than about themselves. This must not be confused with compulsive self-sacrificial martyrdom or compulsive dependency on each other. These are people who really care about each other, and who are really capable of mutual emotional investment, without the annihilation of self or the obliteration of individuality. (They do not make statements like: "Forget about me—anything you want is OK.")

Interparental love (parents who love each other) is

one of the great seeds of health. This is so for several reasons. It provides an active example of adult emotional interchange and makes for an optimistic viewpoint in relating to people. It is a formidable enemy of future cynicism and bitterness. It also provides a humanly warm and secure emotional climate which is extremely important to a lifetime sense of emotional security. These parents, in having, at the least, given their family moments of happiness, have demonstrated to you that marriage and family life can be a happy enterprise.

If you have had parents who loved each other and you know it (don't confuse this with overt sexual acting-out or the *dears* or *honeys* which some people use as easily as they breathe air), then you have a great reserve of strength which can be used in days of adversity. Chances are that these people have demonstrated their mutual concern through action, rather than superficial niceties. This is the guts of it; there is more beer than foam, more cake than whipped cream. These parents, often without intent, have given you a source of inner optimism. This source, when tapped, can make depression and hopelessness short-lived matters. Psychiatrists regard its presence as a very important prognostic entity.

Parents who wanted marriage to each other

These are people who did not feel coerced into marriage. They had the capacity to commit themselves to a long-term, sustained involvement. They were willing to take responsibility for each others' mutual interest in their future lives and well-being. People like this

9

may have at least a modicum of maturity which will provide some of the roots of future family emotional security.

Parents who wanted children

Don't take this one for granted! Some wanted them, some didn't, and it has little to do with planning. Many people don't plan, but unconsciously want children. Some people plan, but do not want them at all. They are only complying with what they think is "right." People who want children are people who like children and who are able to accept them as children (see the next two assets). They do not use their children vicariously—that is, to live through them. They do not use them to compete with their own friends. ("Bill won six medals"; "Mary is a perfect little lady"). They do not expect them to grow up and become precocious, controlled little adults so as to be free of them as soon as possible. They like kids, want kids and expect kids to be kids, and they accept them as such.

Acceptance into the family

Your parents were not disappointed with the sex of their child or any other characteristic. If your mother and father accepted, liked and brought you up as a dark-haired, brown-eyed girl (which in fact you are), then you have an extremely important asset. From the beginning, you have known acceptance for what you basically are. From birth you have had a seed which held the inherent possibility of blossoming into self-acceptance and self-esteem. You have also been blessed with the earliest necessary ingredient for a good sexual identification (you know you are a girl) and a good sexual life.

There are people who prefer a girl or boy or a blond or brunet baby, etc., etc. These people give up these preferences as soon as their baby is born. However, there are other people whose own self-hate and multiple serious problems make for deep-seated, destructive, long-standing prejudices. These people will reject a child who is the wrong sex or looks the wrong way or who acts the wrong way ("not like me"). This rejection can be blatant, subtle or even unconscious, but it is always extremely destructive. I have seen a number of boys dressed as girls and brought up as girls for their first twelve years. The results were very serious, indeed. These parents are planting seeds for future sexual confusion (homosexuality, impotence, frigidity), self-rejection, self-hate, lack of confidence, etc. These children feel unwanted and grow up feeling confused, fragile and vulnerable. They have been "losers" from birth and very often need professional help in order to change.

Parental love for their children—you

This one appears to be a necessary and absolute corollary to interparental love. But it ain't necessarily so! Not all adults are capable of relating to children. Many "act" out a proper parent-child relationship. Intellectually, the thing looks very sound, indeed. But it is only a proper act and deep down, where it counts, the child feels it to be phony. He knows the difference and cannot be fooled by ceremonial acts designed to demonstrate interest and love. I have known any number of parents who spend the majority of their waking hours dragging Maxy from one activity to another and who play at playing ball with him or knitting with Maxine, etc.—deep down hating every second of it. These are people who compulsively feel that parents *should* love and be interested in their kids and who attempt to fool themselves into believing that they are responding to love with much togetherness activity. They are, in fact, responding to a compulsion, to a *should* and not to love at all. They know it and so do the kids. It is very sad to see parents and children compulsively driven from one activity to another without happiness and obviously very sullen, irritable and angry.

More often than not, parents who love and really relate to their children *do just that*. They love and relate! They feel *it* and *it* shows. There is no artificial act. There is no patronizing getting down to his level; nor is there a bullying get up to my level; or a hidden *desire to be emulated* level ("do as I have done"). These are parents who live in a natural and easy parent-child relationship and who are not tormented by a need for constant overt demonstration of their love and interest. These are parents who are not guilt-ridden in feeling inadequate to the responsibility of being adults and are not embarrassed by kids who are kids. They enjoy adult pleasures and accept their children's enjoyment of child pleasures. Here, there is no compulsion to play childish games, nor the inordinate nagging demand that the child somehow ought to grow up in order to free them of this necessity. This one, incidentally, is a destructive bind in which the child cannot win. By demonstration (parent participation in

12

games), he is "told" that it is all right to be a child, but by demonstration (parent irritation or sullenness in participating), he is told that this kind of gaming is an awful nuisance which somehow always evokes hostility.

So what about this, the most crucial seed of all—parental love? First, please remember that this is not a black or white situation. There are degrees, shades, relative values, and many nuances. But if you've had parental love, real love, to any degree, you are in a fortunate position, indeed. It is reported that Sigmund Freud said that his success was only possible because of his mother's great love for him. Clinical observations have taught us that there is great validity in the fact that early roots of self-confidence are generated by a mother's love and confidence in her children, so let's take a good look.

Parental love is not overprotective. The parent does not stifle and constrict her child, preventing growth through healthy experiences in order to allay her own anxiety. The mother or father who "overprotects" often rationalizes that this is done for the protection and good of the child. This, of course, is not so and has a crippling effect, often making the future adult a morbidly dependent, inadequate person whose potential has never been realized in any area. Loving parents have confidence in their children and in their ability to encounter the world and to grow. They are also sufficiently concerned so as to provide appropriate attention and limits during each stage of the formative years. They are not detached from their kids—separated and encapsulated in an adult and impenetrable world. They do not use their children in order to live vicariously through them. They do not attempt to squeeze their kids into preset patterns that are connected to their own aspirations and that have nothing to do with the child's natural characteristics and propensities. They allow and encourage freedom of growth, goals and individuality. They accept the natural urges, temptations, explorations and growing pains of growing up.

These parents (yours, I hope, to some degree) are emotionally attentive; they pay attention to what they feel vis-à-vis what you feel. They are emotionally attuned; they are tuned in, know the score—open to understanding, rather than closed and ever ready to lecture, moralize and judge. The importance of having had parents who were emotionally involved, attentive and attuned (without imposition) cannot be overemphasized. This is the stuff that childhood self-acceptance and future adult self-acceptance spring from. This is *real* parental acceptance, and without it the child is deprived of a measuring rod for his self-evaluation. It furnishes him with an opportunity to see himself in relation to other people and to establish his self-esteem. Of course, this will be very important in all future relationships with Max.

A further word here about the *good* parent or more particularly the *good mother*. To a remarkable extent (considering the general lack of good communication in this world) the good mother is so sensitively attuned that she almost anticipates her child's needs. She communicates with him on a level at once much more sensitive and profound than words permit. Her child is not filled with frustration, anxiety and despair produced by a chronic failure to communicate and to fulfill his needs. To a considerable degree, she innately understands and respects (on a feeling as well as thinking level) her child's moods, desires, needs, assets and limitations. In short, she is not emotionally blocked, distant or cut off from him. She is in close touch with her own feelings which makes for being tuned in to his particular assets and his seeds of health. She *feels for them* and possesses a healthy gratification in seeing them developed without exploitation for her own self-glorification.

Of course, the ideal mother doesn't exist—but to any

extent that she approaches this ideal, you have a most valuable (possibly—after life itself—*the* most valuable) asset.

Parents who provided basic necessities

Not all parents love their children, but some don't provide the basic needs of life, either. Some can't, some won't. Those who can but don't are obviously much more emotionally destructive than those who would if they could. If your parents cared enough for you to work and to provide you with adequate food and shelter then they have at least in some measure demonstrated your importance to them. In so doing, they have initiated self-acceptance and esteem. They have also demonstrated to you the valuable lesson of what it is to have a sense of practical responsibility for other human beings.

Respectful parents

These are parents who treated their children compassionately, honestly, and kept their promises. These parents did not use their authority and "expertise" to bully or to manipulate in and out of situations as a matter of convenience. They respected their children as people, demonstrated this respect with straightforward behavior and in so doing planted in them the seeds for future self-respect, as well as respect for Max.

15

Parental consistency

Your parents were consistent in their values and attitudes toward their children and operated within a consistent frame of reference. This kind of consistency provides an atmosphere which is the antithesis of a jungle-like, potentially danger-ridden, environment. It provides a feeling of stability, security and optimism in regard to the world and people. Inconsistency in this area usually results in inconsistent inner-self demands, in addition to insecurity, self-doubt and distrust for others. Thus, inconsistent values and demands of hypocritical, cynical parents will result in much inner conflict, dividedness and anxiety in an individual who couldn't turn about fast enough to comply with ever-changing parental demands. This makes for great difficulty with decisions and often causes a feeling of literally (emotionally) being torn apart —all of which is the antithesis of working out one's own real values. More about values, and *self*, an all-important commodity, later.

Parents who loved life

Your parents loved life and, by example, taught you to live it, love it, revere it and to treat yourself (a living organism) well and with self-respect. These are people who enjoyed living and showed it. Their household was a happy place, oriented to pleasure at no one's expense and one where laughter and joy were never cause for alarm or guilt, but rather highly cherished commodities.

A child can walk into a house and deep down in his belly know the difference at once. Is it a gloomy, sullen atmosphere with an austerity of good feelings? Or is there warmth, cheer and all the stuff that emanates from people who enjoy being together and *living?*

Peace and emotional freedom

These parents provided a peaceful home atmosphere, but even more important, one in which there was ample opportunity to express emotions and feelings without shame or guilt. In this household, neither a show of anger nor sorrow nor love was cause for alarm. Human emotions, and the demonstration of them, were accepted and well understood. There were no statements made like "Boys shouldn't cry," "Girls shouldn't get angry," and other such emotionally constricting pronouncements. This household will provide you with a rich and invaluable source of human feelings and they will be readily available to you so that you can tap them and use them in relation to Max. These parents will not produce children who as future adults will, in effect, be emotionally repressed, constricted individuals, afraid of feeling and suffering from great deadening of feelings. Such individuals often suffer from uncontrollable emotional explosions which can cause almost irreparable fragmentation. The emotionally constricted household often produces dangerous psyche-shattering emotional

17

time bombs. There are people who spend a lifetime tightly holding back all emotions in fear of going completely to pieces.

Environmental roots

To have lived in one place, or at least not to have moved about excessively, and to have gone to one elementary and to one secondary school is a distinct advantage. People who have moved about a great deal in childhood find it difficult to adjust to adult moves. People who lived in one place and went to one school usually find it easier to adjust to adult moves, other things being equal. This is so because living in one place and going to one school gives the child the needed opportunity to familiarize himself with his environment and friends. This gives him a proper sense of identity and confidence in dealing with his environment. Identity and confidence, as well as a sense of security and well-being, when fed by other necessary later life developments, will be all-important in adjusting to new situations and places and people all of his life. I would like to point out here that environment is much more important to children than it is to adults. Their sense of *who* they are is not yet formed and the formation of *self* is intimately connected to where they are and whom they are with. Therefore, being in one place long enough and with the same people (especially friends) is all-important in developing a feeling of relating to the environment and to developing a *self*. I will talk much more about the all-important concept of *self* in a later section.

Privacy and possessions

You have had the experience of having enjoyed the privacy of your own room, your own bed, and your own possessions, clothes, toys, pets, etc., and parents who respected your need for privacy. This strengthens an early concept of what it is to be an integral individual, and contributes to a growing sense of self. It also contributes to a feeling of independence and to the ability to be alone with oneself and to function. This makes for added security, and it is no surprise that people, who as kids had things of their own, can share more readily than those who never had the opportunity to own anything—privately. A greater sense of self makes interrelating easy and nonthreatening. People who feel that they have little to give are afraid to give even a little for fear that they will be either totally absorbed or depleted and emptied.

If you have had privacy as an adolescent, you are lucky indeed. Adolescents demand privacy and exclusive and solitary ownership because they need it as part of their development. It is important to the further development of feelings for self and strength in self. But it is crucial as a step in adjusting to an independent existence in the adult world in which the adult will have his own wife and his own family and colleagues and friends.

19

Physical strength and vitality

If you have these in large amounts then you are indeed gifted. Even in this computerized space age —vim, vigor, vitality and energy, when properly tapped, can be enormous assets in your behalf. In a society that is more and more intellectually oriented, good health and physical strength are, unfortunately, often overlooked, taken for granted, and neglected—sometimes until it is too late.

If you are attuned to your body and it is a good one, then it can be a great source of pleasure to you. Physical activities and the useful expenditure of energy can be most satisfying and therapeutic. We often forget that, despite intellectual and spiritual values, we are still biological organisms, and a good physiology is an absolute prerequisite in making all else possible.

Sexual identification

Not everybody has a feeling for what it is to be a man or a woman in our society and a sense of appropriate sexual identification.

Don't take this one for granted! There are people who have no idea (emotionally) that there are men, women and differences. There are a good many people who are neither heterosexual nor homosexual and who go through life asexually—that is, leading an almost completely nonsexual life. Many people are confused about "maleness" and "femaleness," but they do feel male or female and have an awareness of what they are sexually. This awareness is a basic prerequisite to a well-adjusted heterosexual life.

Sexual awakening, feeling and desire

Some people know what they are—and I don't mean know with their minds. Nearly everybody knows that. I mean *know* in their feelings about themselves. They *feel/know* what they are. But not all of them are awake enough sexually or developed enough emotionally to have sexual desires. Having the desire for sexual activity is a vital step toward an adult sexual life. In terms of prognosis (that is, future outlook), even a homosexual desire is more hopeful than asexuality. As difficult as it is, and it is very difficult, homosexuality can be changed to heterosexuality more easily than asexuality can be converted to sexuality.

The experience of heterosexual aspirations

A man desiring a woman. A woman desiring a man. An adolescent desiring and feeling sexually inclined toward members of the opposite sex. Yes, if you are any of these, then you are well ahead in having the possibility of developing a warm, human, heterosexual relationship. But that is not all. Having healthy sexual goals is an indication that much else about you and your background is healthy. This is an indication that you have many of the ingredients necessary to self-acceptance, self-esteem and confidence, and the wherewithal to relate successfully to Max (whomever he or she is) on a nonsexual level, as well as in the sexual area, where and when appropriate.

Productive functioning

Do you have a history of some period of fairly well-adjusted behavior, that is, a period of functioning daily with other people in ordinary relationships? That you have the stuff to do this is extremely significant. Having related to people in a fairly productive way for however short a time takes considerable health and indicates much in the *relating to people* department. Are you aware that there are people who have been institutionalized all of their lives, locked in private hells into which there is no entering and from which there is no release?

A pleasant appearance

In our culture this plays an enormous role in initiating relationships. This includes both attractive features and the ability and desire to look well. Good taste in clothes and grooming (without narcissistic compulsive preoccupation) is a definite asset in our society. Do you care about how you look? This, in effect, states that you feel strongly enough about yourself and the world to present yourself favorably.

Exceptional good looks or unusual attractiveness

Don't sell this short just because, "I had nothing to do with it." The fact that you were born good-looking does not make this valuable asset less yours, unless you have made it a source of embarrassment. It is yours, so own it and feel good about it. Good looks in our culture are a very much appreciated commodity and certainly help in almost all kinds of relationships. Because of good looks, many people have been treated exceptionally well all of their lives and as a result have enjoyed unusual self-acceptance and self-esteem. I am not suggesting a narcissistic preoccupation with looks nor do I suggest that other areas of human endeavor and development be neglected. However, I think it is a definite attribute if you know that you are good-looking and do your best to look your best. We have all heard statements like, "that dumb blonde" or "beautiful but dumb." These have no basis in fact and usually spring from projected feelings of ugliness, self-hate, jealousy and envy on the part of the person making the derogatory statements. Most beautiful people (who allow themselves to know and own it) have at least been spared the cynicism and bitterness that comes of feeling ugly and sometimes actually experiencing much rejection. This in itself makes possible more experience in relating to people plus the secondary gains of wisdom and knowledge that come from these relationships. People are, of course, prejudiced against and discriminated against for any number of irrational reasons. Generally, however, homely people have much more difficulty in this department than do exceptionally attractive people.

Sex appeal

There are people who are or are not particularly good-looking (and some who are even homely) who have a charismatic sexual attraction that cannot be denied. Unfortunately some people use this potential asset (as they do others) destructively. However, sex appeal, as an alluring force, can be a considerable asset in relating to people. It is particularly valuable when integrated into the matrix of other assets. Witness the political campaigns waged and won with the help of charismatic sex appeal. Of course, sex appeal used to attract the "right" partner is an invaluable asset indeed. By "right," I mean the person with whom you can have a mutually enriching, satisfactory and sustained sexual relationship.

A sense of humor

You are most fortunate if you can laugh, generate laughter in others, see and have a feel for humorous situations and also laugh at yourself. Humor can mitigate tragedy, hopelessness, depression and hardship. It can also be a source of great enjoyment and happiness. Humor lightens the load and blunts the sting of those difficulties in life that must come to us all.

There are many people who, due to background, have a very poorly developed sense of humor. There are others who have blocked the humor in themselves due to shame and embarrassment. There are some who have been brought up to look upon humor as foolish, frivolous, and even irreverent and sinful. Should these people need psychiatric treatment for severe anxiety or depression, the course of treatment can be exceedingly painful. I have, however, seen people who loosen up and develop in the humor department as their psychotherapeutic treatment and growth progresses. Of course, if you have a well-developed sense of humor, your treatment (should you need it) will be that much easier and more fruitful. Most psychiatrists consider a sense of humor an extremely important characteristic in evaluating a patient for treatment.

Of course, a sense of humor is invaluable in relating to Max. A good part of the satisfaction possible in relating is linked to humor. Without it, relating to Max, whoever he is, would be dull and somber indeed.

Good intellectual endowment

This is obviously a superb asset; however, there are some very important *buts.*

1) Superior intellect undeveloped and untrained will be no more effective than a new broom that stands in a corner—unused.

2) An intellect directed purely to intellectualize

and totally repress, isolate and separate oneself from one's emotional life is being used destructively. Intellect is best used when there is no dichotomy between intellect and emotionale—when one's thinking and feeling are equally available, synchronized and integrated.

3) A neurotic investment of pride in intellect can be an isolating force that leads to difficulty in relating to people. This comes of feeling that all else—other than intellectual endeavor and achievement—is unimportant. However, this kind of overintellectualizing is not confined to people of high intelligence. There are people with splendid intellects who lead total, full, rich emotional as well as intellectual lives. There are people with poor intellects who are almost totally intellectualized, encapsulated and isolated from their fellows.

4) A superior intellect, unless well-integrated into the whole of the human structure and existing with proper self-acceptance and esteem, can be used devastatingly in the service of neurotic self-hate and hating others.

So, superior intellect concomitant with other human assets can be a large plus factor in relating to Max. This is an asset that is most useful in a climate of humility, but don't confuse humility with false modesty (more about this in the next section). This asset is an extremely important one to own, to develop and to use constructively. If you've got it, chances are you know it—so, by all means, own it and be happy that you are smart!

Abstraction ability

The ability to make abstractions and to conceptualize and to memorize are exceedingly important.

Although these qualities are inherent parts of intelligence or intellectual endowment, I note them separately here because you can possess one of the aspects of intelligence in greater degree than the others. Knowing how you function best—with what particular quality—can be useful in choosing an occupation, in developing other areas, etc.

Some people are capable of retaining a vast storehouse of facts. Others can visualize and understand issues and concepts with relative ease. Still others are capable of quick insight and response about the essence of issues small and large. Of course, we all have varying degrees of these abilities in different combinations.

A feeling for psychological phenomena

I do not speak here of great talent in analyzing self or other people or being able to read between the lines, etc., though of course all this is very valuable. I mean a feeling for understanding emotions and human behavior on any level and in any area. For example—can you experience anxiety or hostility and eventually recognize it as such and come to some conclusion about it? If you can, then you have a very important asset which can

27

help you a great deal in relating to Max and in your own psychoanalysis, should you ever undergo analytic treatment. To any extent that you can discern cause and effect in the thoughts, feelings and behavior of yourself and others, you have a very valuable asset.

Orientation

Good orientation in time, place and person or quite simply knowing who, when and where you are in relation to others, is of obvious importance. However, this is one asset I never take for granted, having seen any number of people "quite lost" in this regard.

People with organic diseases of the brain often lose this valuable commodity. They are sometimes no longer able to discern time, place or person. They often do not recognize people they have known all their lives—including themselves. This is often seen in advanced cerebro-arteriosclerosis (hardening of the arteries of the brain). However, a firm sense of self and identification is based on a history of emotional as well as physical health.

Imagination

Imagination is an invaluable asset in helping you to reason and to think through *feeling out situations* and coming to conclusions often on a more deeply valid level than intellectual logic alone permits. This means

that you can envision yourself in situations and in so doing evaluate them. Of course, the ability to imagine is
particularly important in the enjoyment of creative works
and is an absolute requisite in functioning as a creative
worker and artist. Here, as with other assets, much will
depend on general emotional health and integration.
Imagination can be used to constructively discern and
cope with reality and to actively relate to people. On the
other hand, many people live in their imaginations and
lose contact with Max and the real world.

A feeling for imagery and beauty

Are you aware of the beautiful sunset and the
clean, salt smell of the sea? The world is so much
brighter when we have the capacity to enjoy music, art or
poetry.

What a wonderful asset to share with Max whoever
he or she is. It leads to great enjoyment and happiness
in sharing in the wonder and beauty of all that goes on
about you. It also affords you constant sources of enrich-
ment and strength to help mitigate the vicissitudes of life.

Artistry and creativity

So many people have this asset to some degree
in one way or another and so few recognize it, much less
make use of it. Don't be shy about this one. Do you like

to cook? Bring up kids? Fix things? Work in wood? Paint? You needn't be the greatest artist to enjoy working at creating and then feeling the enormous satisfaction in seeing a work completed. Developing a creative skill can provide both great happiness and considerable self-esteem, so please don't sell yourself short on this one. Explore, feel yourself out and take a chance. This may not make you "great," but it will make you more "human," more satisfied with yourself and better able to relate to Max.

Ability to express yourself

The ability to express one's self, that is, any unusual ability to articulate, including familiarity and ability with foreign languages, is very valuable. The ability to verbalize is extremely helpful in relating. Very few people can express themselves with precision and clarity of meaning, let alone with descriptive beauty; very few people have the ability to convey imagery or difficult meanings. If you have this asset, do own and cherish it. This one is extremely valuable in relating to Max, as it enables you to convey how you feel in meaningful, precise and clear language.

Stick-to-it-iveness

This is the ability to stick to any work long enough to see it through to a fruitful conclusion. Don't confuse this most constructive asset with a compulsive need to *stick,* even when sticking is destructive. I speak here of the stick-to-it-iveness required to complete any study or training course or any work goal. Success of any kind is almost impossible without this asset. So take a look at your history. To what extent have you completed anything (a model airplane, a sweater, elementary school, high school, college, a typing course, dancing or swimming instructions, etc., etc.)? Of course, some goals are more complex and difficult than others and require greater perseverance. If you have completed college (any professional training, learning to speak a foreign language), then never, never take this wonderful asset for granted or casually pass it off as a matter of course. Believe it or not, many people are not goal-directed and many more are extremely limited in the *stick-to-it-iveness* department.

Being goal-directed

This one is closely related to the previous asset, but is not exactly the same. It is more general and goes beyond perseverance. People who are goal-directed can tap their feelings and intellects sufficiently to come to a conclusion and to a decision about what they want. They are then able to use this decision in constructively directing their energy toward the attainment of their goals. In short—they are able to use time and energy in their own behalf. I see many people who have not developed this important asset. Again and again, I have interviewed unhappy young adults who are seeking, seeking what, they don't know, in a helter-skelter race, for what, they don't know. In short—they are floundering

—using much energy in being anxious and depressed and unable to direct themselves toward one self-satisfying enterprise or goal.

So if you can come to conclusions about what you want and can use these conclusions as constructive guideposts, you are indeed fortunate. This one asset (like most of the others—but it's especially true here) doesn't exist in isolation. If you've got it, then you must have many, many more concomitant healthy assets, too. To list just a few that it indicates: feeling, tapping feelings, being able to be logical, being self-confident, having an interest in self and taking satisfaction and feeling happy in self-accomplishment.

Education

This includes some degree of education in any area or any dexterity, skill or vocational training. This asset is of obvious importance in earning a living and, in so doing, being better able to relate to people as a useful and respected member of the community. This one also contributes to self-respect, self-acceptance and self-esteem. Knowledge that broadens one culturally has great value as a humanizing effect: that is, making you more appreciative of yourself, people and the world you live in. Knowledge that leads to the possibility of gainful occupation is crucial to one's sense of security, belonging and well-being. So, if you've got some—any—education, don't sell it short; it is very important indeed.

Earning a living

The capacity to get a job, to keep a job, and to function in an economic situation—that is, to earn a living, is, of course, an asset of prime importance in the basic business of keeping alive. It indicates enough integration of all assets so that you are able to put your knowledge, training and skill to active use. It also indicates the considerable health necessary to work, and thus to communicate and relate with other people. Have you any idea of how many people there are who are extremely well-trained but too sick (emotionally) to function in any situation in which other people are involved?

Making a home

The ability to organize a home and to perform the daily tasks necessary to do it is crucial to the welfare of the family. Many people do it, but many people don't —because they can't. Among those who can there are many gradations of effectiveness (I do not suggest perfection). To any degree that you are able to do this (contributing to the care of a household of people), you are demonstrating an all-important asset—a vital link in our whole social, sexual, relating system. If this sounds pretentious, I apologize, but it really is terribly important because the family is the very basis of humanity and civilization. Being the mother, and thus the effective hub

33

of a household, is no small contribution, for you plant the seeds of health in your children and the future's adults.

So please, *please*, don't pass this one off lightly. I hear too many statements like, "Anybody can be a mother," "Anyone can clean a house," "What do I accomplish—some women have careers?" These statements are evidence of self-hate and confusion about the relative importance of different life works. A woman can have, and if she desires is certainly entitled to, a career and professional pursuits. *But* let us not undermine the extreme importance of managing a family. Needless to say (but I'll say it again, anyway), the work that goes into it, the expenditure of energy and the potential creative results and satisfaction are enormous.

The ability to discern the real from the fantastic

None of us is in complete contact with reality. Some of us are not in contact at all. To the extent that you can validate reality—know the real and the unreal— you have a superb asset. Functioning in the real world is a corollary and prerequisite for the good economic investment of emotions, energy and time, and this is the stuff of life itself. Eating a piece of bread and butter is much more satisfying than dreaming of eating nonexistent pie à la mode. To know in which areas we tend to be more realistic and in which we tend to be less realistic is very valuable information. This in itself is a very beneficial asset, and a seed, as it permits us to be appropriately cautious and offers the opportunity of reality growth and development where needed. You may ask yourself how realistic you are vis-à-vis the following:

Yourself—your assets; limitations (energy output is a very important one); abilities; pitfalls; self-confidence; illusions; areas needing growth and development.

Knowing your assets and limitations is exceedingly important. Being aware of your assets gives you the opportunity to use and develop them and also to raise your self-esteem. But in our culture knowledge of limitations is often neglected. This knowledge can lead to work in needed areas and growth. It also can save you from fruitless adventures and the painful results of wasted investments of energy, time and emotions.

People—In evaluating their abilities, are you too naïve; too trusting; too suspicious; do you invest emotion in them too readily; are you too stand-offish with them, etc.?

Money—Do you use it in your behalf realistically? Do you overextend yourself? Overinvest? Does it use you? Look over your past history regarding money and your feelings about it and actions with it.

Self-preservation—Are you aware of what is constructive to you and what is destructive? Do you put yourself into pressured life-jeopardizing situations or are you life-oriented and life-preserving? Do you have the ability to discern danger (look over your past life) and not put yourself in jeopardy needlessly? Are you accident-prone? Do you "somehow" fall into financial straits and have a predilection for entering impossible emotional attachments that cannot possibly result in any reasonable reward or happiness?

Timing and placing—I call this one timing and placing and I mean the active practice of putting yourself in the right place at the right time so that you can extend and enrich your life. There are people who somehow are always misplaced or just a little too late. This is no accident. These people are self-saboteurs responding to hidden or not so hidden self-hate. If you have somehow nearly always managed *time* and *place* in your behalf you can be sure that this is no accident. It comes of a need and desire for self-preservation and self-gratification and is born of a relatively high degree of self-esteem. It could not be possible at all without the special asset of being in touch with time and place reality.

Time—Are you realistic about time? Do you know how long it takes you to do things or do you kid yourself into taking on impossible time-consuming tasks? Are you realistic about time and do you also have the patience to wait, without giving up, for changes to take place and the perseverance necessary to preserve your interests toward the fulfillment of your goals? Can you put off immediate satisfactions but continue in immediate involvements in order to arrive at larger achievements later on? If so, then you have some very important assets indeed.

Temptations—Do you know your threshold (how far you can go)? Which ones you can resist—can't resist—want to resist or don't want to resist? Or do you function as a seeming will-o'-the-wisp—pulled this way and that because you have no idea you are dealing with temptations at all?

Deceptions—Do you have any idea about areas where you tend to deceive yourself, and tend to be hypocritical or given to duplicity or rationalizing, etc? Are you doing anything to change these areas—that is, to stop kidding yourself? If the answer is yes, then you are developing another important asset.

Hope—Can you mitigate pain, suffering, self-hate and depression with hope? Do you know that you can change? Do you know (in your feelings—deep down) that there is almost always a choice? Can you take the count (like a fighter who rests on the canvas until the count of nine) and, if necessary, surrender because you can generate hope about the future? Do you have more hope than hopelessness; more hope for yourself and other people than cynicism and bitterness and total resignation? If so, then you have a very important asset and capacity for knowing reality. This is no Pollyanna-ish outlook. This is reality—people can change and grow and can well afford to be hopeful—and being hopeful is also very much a realistic part of the human condition.

Occupational fulfillment

I refer here to having an occupation that holds the promise of some degree of gratification commensurate with your assets and aspirations. This is a rare commodity and if you've got it you have a very valuable opportunity to enhance your self-esteem. To be disdainful and bored with one's life's work is a constant source of irritation, self-hate and feelings of self-degradation.

To actually work in a capacity that has some degree of self-fulfillment and satisfaction is an example of the process of establishing a healthy growing cycle. You have felt good enough about yourself and your ability to aspire to appropriate goals and to fulfill your aspirations. This fulfillment makes you feel good about yourself and enables you to go on doing fulfilling work. Having this excellent asset is also an indication that you respect yourself enough to use time and energy in the way you "have chosen" and in so doing to accomplish tasks satisfying to you. This is prime stuff to use in the battle to combat hopelessness, cynicism and depression. Clinically and prognostically, it is an excellent sign.

Healthy ambition

The desire to grow and to improve yourself and your lot in life is an indication of hopefulness, self-esteem and, of course, is the very necessary beginning in any effort to change and to grow.

This is a very important asset in combating resignation, stagnation and "quitting." That you have this desire (to grow and improve) puts you in the very middle of life and its vital offerings, whatever your age.

The advantage of youth

If you are young and know (in your feelings about yourself) that you are young, then you have some great advantages. You have that all-important commodity —time—time to live, grow, experience, relate, etc. Hopefully, you also have the flexibility to modify your style of life, whenever to do so is to your advantage. Hopefully, you also have the all-important advantage of good physical health.

The advantage of age

I am not looking through rose-colored glasses. Each age has its own advantages. That you have lived (and functioned) to an advanced age is an indication of considerable physical and emotional strength. Age may also have the advantages of experience, mellowness and tolerance. There is a peace that comes with advanced age, born of "living" and having made philosophical adaptations. Older (and wiser) people often have an excellent sense of reality, as to what is and isn't important. They have the wherewithal to peacefully engage in self-contemplation, as well as exploration (and patience) in relating to other people.

Age does not always bring either peace or wisdom. Much will depend on other assets and their integration or lack of it. Much will also depend on one's life's experience. By the same token, youth does not necessarily mean flexibility and the ability to change. I have seen much rigidity, resignation, cynicism and hopelessness in people of all ages. I have also seen "youthful" flexibility, curiosity, vitality, hope, a desire to grow and become broader and healthier and to relate more successfully in people of all ages.

Frustration tolerance

The ability to withstand frustration with relative equanimity is an all-important asset and is known as "frustration tolerance" among psychiatrists. Since it is impossible to gratify everybody's needs at the same time —especially if those needs and desires are divergent, you can readily see how important this quality is in relating to people. We simply do not live in a world that immediately gratifies our every need and desire. An infant feels that he is the whole world and that the whole world is him. If he feels the physical tension of hunger, he cries and his mother gives him the breast or bottle. He feels that the breast or bottle is part of him—his world— *the world*—and that he controls it as his needs dictate. In time, as he develops his identity and personality—*a self* —he gradually learns to differentiate between himself and the rest of the world. In fact, he learns that his skin is the border between himself and the environment. Hopefully, he is also in the process of learning that the outside world (world outside of himself, that is, the environment) is sometimes gratifying and sometimes frustrating. Hopefully, he is learning as he develops, to accept frustration, to tolerate it and to live with it. Again, this frustration tolerance will be linked with the existence and with the development and integration of all his assets. Much will depend on his sense of security and realistic relating as a child. Has he been overindulged and made to feel like a "special person"? Much of this quality will depend on how much he has evolved out as an adult— that is—how much he has grown since his infancy. Much of it will depend on his ability to realistically perceive himself and the world, and himself in the world. Does he unrealistically see himself (as the infant does) as the center of the world—as the world itself and, in a megalomanic way, demand immediate gratification from the world and therefore from himself? If so, he is grossly underdeveloped and in serious trouble. His relations with people will always be grossly disturbed and he will constantly be disappointed with himself and his inability to get what he takes for granted is coming to him. This can lead to massive self-hate, depression and prejudice against others who don't immediately gratify his infantile needs. You can readily see why psychiatrists view frustration tolerance with such seriousness.

If you have a good ability to withstand frustration, this indicates you have considerable health and emotional evolvement as an adult. If you can "wait" and even, if necessary (and better for you), give up certain desires, without self-hate and hating others, this indicates an important emotional integration. This is the stuff that makes the give-and-take that goes on in human emotional exchange possible. In short, this quality in some degree is essential to all adult relationships, in all areas.

The ability to be alone with yourself

This means that you enjoy people but also enjoy your own company. That you regard yourself as a human being and worthwhile company is an indication of much health. Not all people do. Some are terrified to be alone because alone is really alone—to them, it means

41

being with *nobody* at all—and as such is an indication of very low self-esteem.

The ability to be alone *with* yourself and to be self-energizing, self-stimulating and self-igniting—the ability to be either active or passive when alone but to know freedom from boredom and anxiety—at once makes you independent, self-reliant and thus a more mature, as well as an easier person with whom to have a relationship.

Enjoying people

The ability at times to be gregarious—to enjoy people and company—is an obvious asset and not at all mutually exclusive of the ability to be alone. But don't confuse this with a compulsive need to be with people. I would also like to say that I see no virtue in having to play the role of life of the party—to be the most popular, etc. I speak here of being able to be alone and also at times deserving and enjoying the company and camaraderie of other people.

The ability to tolerate anxiety

This asset cannot be stressed too much. Anxiety must come. We all feel nervous, tense and unduly upset at times. Symptoms will vary from the physical to the purely psychological: palpitations, headaches, stomach upsets, insomnia, feeling fearful without apparent cause, etc. *But* the ability to accept and tolerate anxiety will prevent the development of all kinds of destructive, neurotic strategems (to combat the anxiety) and will prevent the snowballing effect of getting anxious about being anxious. You will not run off and do destructive things and get into destructive enterprises in response to panic generated by anxiety. Even more important—the ability to tolerate and to accept anxious feelings can lead to a constructive opportunity. To be able to allow yourself to become anxious, to sit with your anxiety long enough to detect its source, and to enter into the mood of the moment and to work through to some understanding (and insight about your responses to anxiety-provoking situations) is to grow in constructive understanding of your self. Again, this ability comes as part and parcel of all other healthy aspects of self.

For psychiatrists it is invaluable not only in evaluating prognosis, but also as a very important requisite to treatment. Psychotherapy—especially of an analytic nature—is designed to remove neurotic defenses, to confront one with hidden conflicts, hidden truths and the irrationalities of a lifetime, all of which result in ultimate insight, choice about one's self and one's course in life, health and growth. But the process generates anxiety and anxiety is often the growing pain of psychiatric treatment. This anxiety is used by the analyst as a pathway or a guiding light to hidden difficulties and mysteries. You can, therefore, readily see how important the level of anxiety tolerance is in determining the pace, technique and nature of the treatment course with a particular patient.

To feel

This includes the ability to feel emotion and to know it and to be able to express it—that is, to be able to emote—to show others how you feel and what you feel. Have you felt good, bad, anger, love? Have you expressed your feelings to others? This asset is important in knowing who you are in relation to yourself and to others. What you feel is crucial in knowing who you are, what your values are, where you are going, and in retaining the center of gravity for your life so that you have a choice about your life's decisions and actions and are not a will-o'-the-wisp. Feeling and emoting permit you to react, to communicate and to relate to people.

The ability to emote is also crucial to mental health. Without it one's health is indeed in jeopardy. He becomes a walking emotional time bomb and an easy victim of feelings and aspects of himself from which he is cut off. The ability to express both love and anger, without guilt and embarrassment, is all-important in relating. Repressing anger usually leads to repressing love as well. Anger, repressed, often leads to cold, sullen moods, and eventually to vindictive reactions that result in a breakdown in communicating and relating. When people can allow themselves to express anger warmly and appropriately, they can clear the air, communicate, and go on relating and living.

Individuals must at times become disgruntled with each other. This is normal and natural, but reparations, accommodations and mediation cannot be effected without communication of the displeasure and feelings, whatever they are. If you have the ability to talk things over,

44

you are ahead, indeed; but I mean more than verbalizing. By *talking*, I mean to *feel*, to be in touch with your feeling and to be able to communicate what you feel. Of course, this asset is only possible as a concomitant of much security and health. It is, therefore, a very good indicator of one's mental health status. However, it will also be closely related to one's background and upbringing. If as a child you lived in a house where emotions were expressed appropriately and freely without punishment or repercussion, then you already have a considerable start toward further developing this important capacity.

If you are at all inclined to take this one for granted, please be aware that there are many people who are almost completely alienated from their feelings, who can't remember ever having had any feelings, who are emotionally estranged from themselves and all other people, who suffer from a deep inner deadness and spend their lives in a vast emotional vacuum.

Doing—for self and others

Deriving satisfaction from doing things for yourself (in your behalf) and deriving satisfaction from doing things for others complement each other. Indeed, it's almost impossible to have one and not the other. This asset is a very important source of happiness as well as an important component of human interchange and relating. There are people who because of intense self-hate derive no pleasure in giving or doing for either themselves or others.

45

Money—and using it constructively

If you have money you obviously have a valuable asset. But do you know *how* valuable (potentially) in terms of human relating? Many people lose touch with the fact that money represents time, human energy and productivity. As such, an exchange of money is, in effect, an exchange of human effort and thus represents a universal communicating and relating activity. Using money practically and healthfully in a noncompulsive, free-flowing, but appropriate way, is always linked to much else that is healthy and constructive in the way you relate to yourself and to others. Contempt and disdain for money, overawe and worship of money, chronic money entanglements and problems, are all evidence of serious counterparts existing in other areas of emotional interchange.

Sexual experience

Any heterosexual experience, however brief or fleeting or however lacking it may have been in a sustained emotional exchange, is vital. That you had the desire, were able to do something about it, and had an actual sexual encounter with a member of the opposite sex is a "healthy" reflection of the past and at the least portends the possibility of a healthy sexual future.

Sexual and emotional exchange

This means a sustained, satisfying, hetero-sexual encounter, including a mature emotional exchange. Here again, we speak in relative degrees. Sex, like all else between human beings, is never perfect. But there are varying degrees of satisfaction. If you have a history of good sexual adjustment, this is an indication of much health. The sexual lives of people are intimately con-nected with the ways in which they live, relate and ex-change emotions. Difficulties in relating will always have reflections in one's sexual attitudes and practices. The ability to have a sustained sexual relationship, to enjoy sex and to enjoy giving enjoyment through sex, are extremely significant characteristics in an overall person-ality evaluation. In short, sexual success (not to be con-fused with infantile conquests or purely physical achieve-ments, such as multiple orgasms, etc.)—mature sexual involvement and caring for one's self and for a person of the opposite sex—is always linked to success and the possibility of more success and growth in other areas of human endeavor.

Liking people

This must not be confused with a compulsive need to like everyone and to see everyone as a "nice guy" or with a compulsive need to be liked. I mean that if you

47

are a person who genuinely likes people (especially children), then you undoubtedly like yourself, too—perhaps much more than you suspect. This is most important in relating to yourself and growing and in relating to other people. This is also an indication of optimism and hope about people—including yourself.

Honesty as a policy

I do not mean a compulsive, posed honesty. Real honesty is an indication of considerable self-esteem, self-trust, and trust for and openness with other people. This makes deep relating a very real possibility, as honesty is a requisite to a real emotional interchange, to feeling for each other—to caring. There are people who, under the guise of honesty, are always telling other people things that barb and hurt them. This is honesty used in the service of vindictiveness; it is compulsive and posed—born of sickness rather than health.

Creativity and special skill

Any special creative or artistic ability, like painting or writing or composing or playing an instrument or an athletic skill, is immediately satisfying in terms of self-accomplishment, expression and self-esteem. This valuable asset is also a prime way of relating to

other people. Art—any art, including the art of athletics
and the lively arts—is a way of conveying feelings. An
art work may well convey the deepest feelings of all—
feelings that we have all had—and that are conveyed
from generation to generation and from place to place.
I like to think of art as a relating process between the
artist through his work, and *his viewers, listeners, readers
or spectators.*

Charm

This asset must not be confused with duplicity
("conning"), manipulation and machination. No amount
of phony acting can simulate it. This one is for real and
a great asset in all encounters. Don't ask me what it is,
because I don't know. But some people certainly have
this charismatic quality and I certainly do know when
I'm in its presence. When it's the real thing, nearly everybody will agree in their recognition of it.

Human encounter

Any involvement with another human being
anytime in life—however fleeting an encounter—can be
considered the basic unit of human relatedness. Don't
take it for granted—there are people who have always
been too ill to be involved with anybody at all on any
level whatsoever.

49

Human involvement

A deep relationship with someone in your living experience means having had a sustained relationship in which you and the other person communicated enough to get to know each other (how you felt) and in which you cared enough about each other to exchange feelings, to share experiences and to be concerned with each other's welfare.

This, of course, could not take place at all unless there is a history of considerable health. Its possibilities as a seed of health are enormous.

Empathy

The ability to identify with, to sympathize and to empathize are more of the assets constituting the actual process of relating. This enables you to feel for the other person's position and to care and even to be compassionate—all very important assets in successful relating. Again, these will be most helpful if used constructively and as part of a pattern of other constructive actions and uses of self.

Loving and being loved

I speak here of the experience of loving and being loved, but not necessarily on a sexual level. Did you ever feel love for anybody or feel that anybody felt love for you? This is evidence of having the ability to love and it has in effect proved to you that you are lovable. There are people who feel that they are absolutely unlovable. This feeling causes them to be very suspicious of people's expressions of love, warmth and admiration, and is extremely destructive to a "winning" relationship.

The experience of love in childhood (and lovability) is extremely important to proper development in all areas. It is particularly important in establishing a love fund experience to be tapped and developed in later life. A childhood experience of complete love depletion is very serious prognostically. It is a guarantee of many serious personality and relating complications. It is also exceedingly difficult to establish the ability to love and the feeling of lovability for the first time in adulthood.

Feeling intensely

Do you have a history of intense feeling about anything, any issue, any activity, or anybody at any time in your life? Baseball, tropical fish, a girl, a boy, an author, a philosophical belief—it's all good stuff, and very important. Why? Because it shows ability to feel intensely, to

51

generate strong emotion and interest and to invest something or someone outside yourself with your emotion strongly enough so that you feel it intensely. Dedication to winning on any level, in any area, requires an intensity of emotional investment. Unfortunately, there are scores of people who cannot make the investment—who cannot feel strongly about anything.

Contentment

This includes the experience of happiness or contentment for any period of time at any time in your life. Of course being happy, at all happy—feeling good—comfortable with one's self and others—is something we all strive for in many ways and it is too often an elusive, but wonderful human enterprise and experience. But here, too—like love—if an adult's history is completely lacking in this experience, the prognosis is very serious. Many experiences of contentment—and I don't mean resignation and feeling anesthetized or dead, I mean being happy, feeling good—are an indication of great security about one's self and much overall health.

The capacity to develop new interests

Have you recently become interested in new people, things, causes, ideas, concepts?
This is an all-important indication of aliveness, flexi-

bility and growth. Of course, I refer here to constructive interests leading to self-development and successful and happy relating to Max.

Good judgment

The ability to form appropriate judgments, through feelings, logic, comparison, use of past experience and research is invaluable in being a winner. Look over your past. Sure, there have been errors in judgment—some bad ones. But how many times have you been right—about love, business, schooling, buying a house, etc. Don't take them for granted. This ability is an indication of integration and adult growth and development, and is directly linked to appropriate realistic behavior. Since it is intimately linked to one's general ability in discerning reality, you can readily see its importance in psychiatric evaluation, as well as in evaluating relating to Max.

Teaching ability

This is the particular verbal ability to communicate difficult ideas and concepts. There are people who are good "teachers," who can explain and describe and use words to convey understanding and feelings, who can clarify, stimulate, open new doors. This is, of course, a superb winning asset, no matter who Max is.

Self-assertion

This is the ability to assert yourself, to stand for something, to support your opinions or feelings according to the particular values which are distinctively yours. This is one of the principal constituents of self in relating to Max.

Humility

Don't confuse this most valuable and human asset with the self-effacement and false modesty which often mask great pride and arrogance. The person with true humility is well aware of and in touch with his assets, values and self. It takes enormous security and self-esteem to have humility, and it takes enormous self-respect and respect for one's endowments to respect other people, especially those with lesser endowments. People with true humility are philosophically and emotionally mature people.

Owning your assets

I speak here of the all-important asset of knowing your assets and owning them. We have listed and discussed some important assets—they are interdependent and interrelated and so they overlap and at times the information about them is repetitious. But go over them—each and every one—neglect none! The list can of course go on and on. Most of us possess some seeds of health. No one person possesses only healthy aspects or all of them. I repeat—learning to nurture the seeds with which we are endowed will help immeasurably vis-à-vis Max. I repeat—the act of living itself is daily and visible evidence of enough inner health to survive, to function and even to relate to Max successfully.

There are many more assets and seeds of health. Ferret them out! Don't deny them in false modesty. Being open to discovery of them in yourself will provide excellent long-life therapy which will be passed on to your children. This will give you an added opportunity to plant some of the seeds in them.

So, own those that you've got. Adopt all those that you can discover and you will be able to compensate for those that you can't have.

Ownership is all-important! If you really own what you've got, nobody but nobody can take *it* away from you! Knowing your assets and owning them will make you feel less fragile, less vulnerable and so much freer and healthier in relating to Max.

SECTION II

Muddles

Muddles are confusions, misconceptions, binds and blocks, traps and prejudices, stereotypes and vicious cycles. They have one thing in common. They are all extremely destructive in relating to one's self and in relating successfully to Max. Many muddles are not experienced consciously. We are not aware of them. But they are there and because we don't recognize them and therefore exert no control over them, they are even more destructive than those of which we are vaguely aware.

Muddles cut us off from our resources—our assets—and they constantly confuse and destroy any possibility of success in relating to Max. Muddles are the cornerstones of being a loser! They are the very stuff that losing is made of. Clarification and insight destroy muddles.

In this section, I will describe some very important muddles and attempt to clarify them. Please work hard on these with me. In addition to the obvious benefit derived from the clarifications we make, the exercise will enable you to recognize other muddles. In so doing, you will learn to clarify them yourself and to grow in a healthy, winning, happy direction.

Strength and weakness

Again and again, I see patients who say, "So and So is a strong person." After a good deal of probing, I find out that "So and So" has most of the following characteristics: He is stubborn, rigid, domineering, attempts to impose his will on others, never or nearly never compromises, is almost completely unyielding, is opinionated, successfully hides softer feelings; is capable of a show of anger and vindictiveness; can use the truth "to tell people off"; is very competitive; acts like a bull in a china shop; is relatively uncaring about other people's feelings. He can be pompous, quarrelsome, egotistical, pedantic, demagogic and patronizing. Sooner or later the same patient goes on to say, "Jim is a weak person." As it turns out, Jim has a combination of the following characteristics: He can change his mind, accept inconsistencies in himself and in others; he can express emotions including tender, gentle, soft feelings; he is capable of sentimental displays; he can weep in the presence of other people; he is considerate of other people's feelings and does not use the truth to hurt; he lives and lets live, not imposing his will on others, and he is generally looked upon as good-natured.

This particular muddle—the confusion about strength and weakness—is extremely prevalent and very destructive. It fosters attempts to idealize and to emulate characteristics which have a weakening rather than a strengthening effect. It also fosters destructive relationships and very disappointing emotional investments and attachments.

What is strength and what is weakness? I speak here of emotional strength, the kind that enables you to be a winner with Max and life generally.

Emotional strength is, of course, intimately linked to and largely comprised of the integrated assets and seeds of health previously discussed. The strong person is sure enough of himself (who he is and what he stands for) so that he does not have to gather synthetic strength through the manipulation of other people. He is strong enough so that he does not have to cling tenaciously to a once-established argument, position or vested interest. He knows (with his feelings—in his guts) that his identity is so well established that he can change his ideas and concepts without being threatened with a feeling of non-being. This enables him to adapt readily to new situations, concepts and people without the compulsive need for complete mastery. He can live and let live. He does not have to establish his own position again and again by beating you over the head with it. He emotes readily—unafraid of feelings, whatever they are, and unafraid of people learning of his feelings. He is strong enough so that he need not make a show of "never getting hurt" or feeling hurt. He does not have the need to compulsively detach himself from any possibility of meaningful involvement in order to feel safe. He does not have the need to compulsively mirror and comply with other people's opinions and needs in an attempt to be universally liked—and safe. People simply do not threaten him. He is sufficiently expressive and at home with his emotions so that he does not operate like an emotional time bomb. He can live with adversity without a huge self-hate or hate-others reaction. He has the ability to feel bad, even depressed, and to bounce back and to make a go of it. Like the flexible branch of a tree, he can bend this way and that and still be himself without breaking.

The weak person has a poor concept of who he is, what he stands for, and what his values are. He feels that an emotional investment on his part will leave him depleted, empty and vulnerable. He feels that he must either remain at a distance or be visibly compliant so that people will like and not hurt him, or that he must master every situation and person, because the world is a threatening jungle full of potential danger from anyone who might get the upper hand. Of course, he will, with probing, reveal a combination of all these compulsive ways of relating to people. Karen Horney indicated that one of them (compliancy, mastery or detachment) will probably be in ascendency and thus will be more immediately apparent. In this individual, there will be little flow of real emotionale and little investment of feeling in causes, people, etc., based on real values and self, rather than on the compulsive need to escape potential danger. This individual's ways are set and rigid and he finds change difficult and shows little or no evidence of ability to adapt to new or unfamiliar situations. Thus, this person is often demagogic and pedantic and rigidly stubborn, giving the impression of powerful beliefs, but really suffering from powerful fears. Stress and strain are not well tolerated and in this case the rigid inflexible twig breaks when called upon to bend "too much," too quickly.

Aggression and self-assertion

People constantly confuse these two—lump them together and usually (in our culture) view them as healthy. *Aggression* is a compulsive neurotic action based on a need to put somebody or something down. If traced, you will find that this need invariably stems from a feeling of weakness and the feeling of being threatened in some way. This threat is usually felt as potential danger to one's pride. Remember, and this is all-important—neurotic aggression is choiceless—the individual *must* strike out and cannot say "I won't." This aggression is often masked and rationalized as healthy self-assertion, but it is no such thing. The aggressive person looks like he certainly knows who he is and what he stands for, and he appears to have a willingness to do something about it. This is not true. If it were true, he would not have to put anyone else down (to overreact) in order to substantiate his shaky beliefs and lack of self-confidence. An aggressive act is often followed by self-hate, fear of repercussion or reprisal, and guilt.

Self-assertion is not related to any action against anyone else. It is born of a real feeling for one's self, identity and values. There is a desire (not an absolute need) to express one's self or to get something for one's self, etc. There is a choice in that the individual doesn't feel that he "must" assert himself. There is no feeling that his pride or his life is threatened or required to be at stake. Since there is no vindictive need to bang up against anybody or to put anybody down, there is no associated fear of repercussion or feelings of guilt.

Doing for self and selfishness

I see this confusion again and again. There are many people—especially self-effacing and compliant people—who feel that any desire, need or wish or action in one's own behalf or for one's own gratification and pleasure is an act of selfishness. They feel that this in some magical way takes something away from somebody else. Since they see any act on the part of other people which is not immediately altruistic and self-sacrificing as being selfish, you can readily envision the resulting confusion and the disastrous complications in relating to Max.

The *Talmud* says: "If I am not for myself who will be? If I am only for myself what am I?" The point is that one cannot be for other people without being for one's self and one cannot be for one's self without being for other people. The *Talmud* long ago recognized the value of self-respect in dealing with others. We are all part of this world—ourselves and other people—and in doing for ourselves, we are also doing for this world and the people it contains. In doing for others, we are also involved in doing for self through the personal satisfaction derived from relating to others in this way. Doing for self and doing for others are therefore never mutually exclusive and constantly complement and supplement a continuing human process.

The individual who confuses doing for self with selfishness must be compulsively altruistic and often must make sure that everybody else gets something before he can have it. This more often than not leads to his not getting it at all. This invariably leads to great resentment. Since this person cannot admit anger (because it destroys his image of saintliness), he represses it and is often unaware that it is there. But it is there and precisely because it is hidden and beyond his control it produces great damage in his relating to Max.

Selfishness involves a compulsive preoccupation with one's self to the exclusion of others. Immediately, it is a clinically emotional disturbance preventing an individual from being concerned with or doing for others. Ultimately, it results in a deprivation of the gratification derived from any kind of deeper relationship with others. This in turn prevents a real emotional doing and nourishing of one's self and produces a stultifying self-preoccupation. The individual thus afflicted usually deprives himself in most areas and generally operates in an emotionally tight and constricted way. Of course, the results in relating to Max are highly destructive, but the person in question has no choice. He cannot choose to give or not to give, to do or not to do. He simply cannot! Doing for others, giving to others is terribly threatening inasmuch as he feels that he has little or nothing to give and must hoard all that he thinks he has in order to survive. Individuals suffering from severe forms of selfishness are usually quite narcissistic and feel separated from the rest of the world and even encapsulated in a private world of their own.

The fear of being crazy and being crazy

The fear of being or becoming crazy is one of the most prevalent fears of all and one that many people have but don't talk about. Nearly everybody is a little crazy—or neurotic—and at times more neurotic than at other times. Then there are people who are psychotic and in whom there is severe impairment of contact with reality and with Max. Compared to people who are afraid of going crazy and all of us who are a little crazy, there are very few psychotic people and they, too, can get relatively well.

Well, what about the fear of going crazy? Generally, we find that it is not at all directly related to what is actually neurotic or "crazy" in an individual. We also find that different people have different concepts of what crazy is and what is crazy about them. In almost all cases, we find that the "craziness" is linked to aspects of themselves and feelings, the existence of which they try to deny. In some cases, this denial has been successful enough so that there are whole areas which are unknown and unfamiliar to the individual in question. Sudden confrontation with hitherto unheard from and unfamiliar feelings, desires, impulses and needs is interpreted as going

65

crazy and often creates painful anxiety and even panic. Thus, we may see the expansive, overbearing, controlling individual who suddenly finds out he is a very dependent person, too, seeing himself as going "soft" and mad. This may happen suddenly, such as at the time of the death of a mate on whom he has depended for years without being aware of it. The compliant, self-effacing individual who sees herself as angelic and all-loving and lovable may see herself as going crazy in the midst of a great but normal and appropriate display of anger. The detached person who has much pride invested in "noninvolvement with people or causes" may fear an attack of craziness on signing a long-term contract, feeling suddenly closed in and "choked." Of course, incidents and degrees of reaction will vary from subtle, fairly well-hidden fear to blatant terror. We can understand this terror if we realize that an individual is almost, in effect, suddenly confronted with the possibility of being another person or losing his identity or self. But he is not losing himself. In fact, he is extending himself, adding more of his hidden self to his open self; he is growing and has the chance to become healthier. This is not craziness at all. Craziness is more related to closing off more and more of self and establishing more and more distance between one's self and the rest of the world. It involves great distortions in perceiving reality which are manifested by fantastic delusions and hallucinations.

So—fear of craziness is not craziness! Dissipating this fear is very important in permitting us to be more of ourselves and to have more of ourselves to relate to Max with.

"Knowing" and "feel/knowing"

I speak here of knowledge or knowing of anything, any concept, any person, one's self, and particularly Max, the particular person to whom you are relating. I hear people say, "I know" or "I understand" and they really think they do. Patients in the course of psychoanalytic treatment eventually find out that there is knowing and *knowing*. They start knowing or understanding something about themselves or Max and eventually find their knowing change in timbre and quality as it becomes a deep, profound, more encompassing, meaningful thing. Superficial knowing born of intellectual and good logical rationale and reasoning can be valuable. But it can also be destructive if it is confused with deeper levels of knowing. This deeper level of knowing is invariably more valuable because it has more validity and is, therefore, more reliable. Let us call this deeper knowing *"feeling/ knowing."* If you *feel/know* something or something about someone, then you can readily count on it. Now why is this so? Or better yet, what is this feeling/knowing about? This knowing, feeling/knowing, springs from an integration of all that goes on in you, including all of your feelings, your past experiences with yourself and other people, your deep emotional insights in regard to past and present issues as well as your combined values. It is comprised of the very stuff that makes you uniquely *you*. In short, it comes from the encounter of the essence of you with whatever or whomever you wish to feel/know. To feel/know—the deepest knowing of all—you cannot will yourself to know. You must be ready and open to use your total self as the exquisitely sensitive instrument it is

67

vis-à-vis the knowing you wish to acquire. This takes much development of self plus the passage of time. It occasionally happens that you feel/know in a flash, but it is much more common for considerable time to pass so that you know and know and know and finally *really* know in your guts—feelingwise—more profoundly than with logic. You are on a really insightful *total* level. So— don't sell you or a concept or Max short. You may be very quick-minded and you may *know* very quickly. But don't pass this off to yourself as feel/knowing. Let things develop, let yourself tap you in all your resources, give yourself time so that you can arrive at feel/knowing knowledge which will provide you with the most valuable insights.

100 percent passes

This is the black or white, all or nothing outlook. Many, many people see themselves and other people this way, with little or no awareness, and then they can't understand why they are miserable, terribly critical of Max and incapable of successful relating. Wherever they meet Max—in business, marriage, as parents—they are invariably disappointed and dejected.

For these people, total success is of paramount importance, and in order to pass or for those they "test" (and they are constantly testing) to pass, 100 percent just about does it. Everything is extreme—at opposite poles—either 100 percent one way or the other. It is "good or bad" with no in-betweens or gradations. In short, they are the victims of the essence of a stringent and sick environment that teaches, extolls and pressures people to achieve the impossible. This environment says little or nothing of self-acceptance and acceptance of Max on the basis of relative degrees of achievement and passing, let alone occasional and inevitable failures. While there are people who function almost solely in this extreme and destructive way, we all do this to a certain degree and ought to be aware of this most destructive phenomenon.

This kind of perfectionistic black and white outlook removes us from the real world of many shades of gray and many gradations of quality. It makes us malcontent, angry, self-rejecting, self-hating, cast-off, overdemanding and just plain miserable. It also has a constricting, inhibiting and even paralyzing effect which simply stated goes like this: Since I can't do it perfectly, I won't do it at all. This results in failure because of the failure of effort. I have seen adolescents fail because they did not study, and subsequent probing pointed out that they did not study because they knew they couldn't learn it "all." Besides, they could then tell themselves that at least the failure wasn't due to stupidity but to a lack of study instead. In a really crazy way, there is also occasional pride taken in receiving a complete but "perfect" failure, rather than a near but "imperfect" pass. So are you overdemanding of yourself and others? Do you live in a black and white world of fail or pass? Are you constantly disappointed with friends who don't turn out to be *everything* you expected; do you see your children as disrespectful because they are not 100 percent obedient? Please remember that all issues, quantities and qualities have many gradations and this includes success with self, people and all endeavors.

Talking and communicating

I use the terms communicate and relate almost interchangeably. Communicating, to me, connotes the conveyance of information or ideas, as well as feeling/knowing. Therefore, talking and communicating are not necessarily the same thing. Again and again I have seen people "talking" to each other without giving one another any information, any aspect of self, any aspect of feeling. They each mouthed words, articulated and sometimes enunciated beautifully, without conveying a single idea and without changing one another, in any area, one iota. I have also seen people talk and use words of the same language who obviously did not understand each other. For them, the same words had different nuances and even different meanings. They obviously came from a world of different experiences and their frames of reference were totally unfamiliar one to the other. With each word, they misunderstood each other, and they compounded that misunderstanding and widened the gulf between them even though they had actually started out in complete agreement.

I have seen people who hardly talk at all who are obviously in excellent communication. They are open to each other, receive each other, operate on the same wavelength, so that it takes a minimum of verbal symbols—words—to convey meanings, ideas, feelings, and subtle nuances. These people relate—tell each other how they feel—and invariably have enough impact on one another so that both have changed because of their talk (verbal or relatively nonverbal). These people, through their communicative encounter, have changed each other, have been changed, and thus have effected that most basic and important rudiment of human existence. They have had a mutual exchange of human understanding and have thus grown and extended their worlds and in a way can never be the same again. Communicating is certainly not a black or white activity. There are many gradations and many varieties. But it is certainly the antithesis of compulsive small talk, chatter and the mouthing of many words, which people often mistake for some kind of attempted communication. So, people talk and communicate; people don't talk or talk relatively little and communicate, and people do and don't talk and don't communicate. I'd like to point out that communication can be extremely subtle. It can take place on a practically nonverbal level without the people involved knowing that they are doing it or knowing how they are doing it. This is especially true of people who want to communicate, who are open to themselves and to what goes on in themselves and who want to share. These are almost always people who have had common or similar experiences and a common frame of reference. For these people, a shrug, a grunt, a gesture, an expression, even silence itself, can be meaningful. If you are particularly interested in communication and relating you might read *I and Thou*, by the late Jewish philosopher Martin Buber, and the first part of the book *Character Analysis* by William Reich. I consider the first part of the book invaluable to people interested in human behavior. I feel that the second part is, unfortunately, completely unrealistic.

Where there is much verbiage and little or no communication, you will often find a great deal of anxiety and tension. Many people talk a great deal as a way of getting rid of anxiety (excessive mouth movement—like people who overeat when they are anxious). Many people talk in a futile attempt to reach somebody else and to be

71

reached, so as to feel less empty, less dead and less removed from their own feelings. Many overtalk in order to be reassured, as a way of attempting to be liked, and many overtalk to convince themselves of something that they themselves do not believe deep down. Others talk to mask real feelings—really as a way of fending people off, keeping many, many words between themselves and other people because the closeness of people is threatening to them. Very verbal people are not necessarily interested in people or in communicating with them. Of course "overtalking" can also be considered a form of communication. But it is at best a compulsive activity born of neurotic need and is not to be confused with a healthy desire (and choice) to communicate and to relate.

In view of all that we have discussed up to now it is sometimes very valuable to stop during a conversation or a discussion and to seriously "listen" to oneself and the other person or persons involved. This may be the only way to find out whether anything is happening and if so, what. If nothing is happening or the gulf is getting wider, it may be best to stop altogether or to stop for a while, to go slower. It might be best to approach the situation in a different way entirely. Were you ever involved in a particular solution to a math problem and somehow went on and on, in the firm, but erroneous impression that this was the correct approach? Perhaps you found out much later (after the expenditure of much time and effort) that you had gone up a blind alley, whereupon a completely different approach quickly solved the problem. This is also true in communicating with people (especially people of divergent generations, adult vis-à-vis adolescent) but—

1) You must be aware of the muddle—words or talk-

ing and communicating are not necessarily mutually inclusive or exclusive.

2) You must want to communicate, rather than just make words or sounds.

3) You must be open to evaluating the process going on between you-and-you and you-and-Max.

4) You must be willing to use and tap all of yourself in order to modify the process if necessary, even if this means using unfamiliar ways and methods and even being creative in new and fresh attempts.

That which is masculine and that which is feminine

This one really makes people miserable. People think of nearly everything as one or the other and this includes clothes, customs, ways, gestures, things (the French *le* and *un*—masculine, and *la* and *une*—feminine, label everything sexually) and, more important, interests and feelings. The confusion about what is male and what is female leads to a fear of acceptance of any feeling that is deemed to be of the opposite sex. This leads to rejection of whole areas of self and to underdevelopment of the rejected areas. Emergence of unwanted feelings leads to fear of homosexuality and even panic, as well as to great destruction of self-esteem and is, of course, disastrous in relating successfully to Max.

As a psychiatrist I have been asked a particular question again and again. It usually goes like this: "Why are homosexual men so much more talented than heterosexual or normal men?" The answer is that they are not more talented, but do, in fact, give that illusion. Here is why.

73

Men who are resigned to homosexuality—that is, who lead an active homosexual existence, feel that they do not have to reject their "feminine" feelings, tastes, proclivities and activities, nor are they reluctant to express these feelings in terms of art, decorating, dancing, etc. This results in making use of many areas of self and many feelings which the heterosexual male (and his counterpart in the female) carefully keeps under wraps. Many men and women cannot make use of, let alone express, much that they feel, because their feelings have a connotation of homosexuality. Homosexuality is not an inborn malformation, but rather a symptom. It is a symptom of serious emotional disturbance. People so afflicted (except for the acceptance of "wrong" feelings) are not nearly as well-developed emotionally (and in the potential talent department) as their normally sexed confreres.

What about what is seen as maleness and what is seen as femaleness? Let me point out that we are not always consciously aware of our attitudes. But let me remind you again that the less awareness we have, the more effect and destruction the confusion will have. When I say anti-, this will vary from person to person; from weak anti-male (or anti-female) attitudes to very strong feelings about what is anti-male or female.

Feelings—just having them is seen as an anti-male thing. This applies tenfold to softer feelings and twentyfold to the *expression* of feelings, especially sorrow or pain or regret or sympathy or sentiment in the way of tears. *Lack of interest in sports* is seen as anti-male. *Being dependent on other people*—anti-male. *Difficulty asserting self*—anti-male. *Shyness*—anti-male. *Interest in ballet* —anti-male. *Interest in furniture arrangement, cooking, knitting, etc.*—anti-male. *Anti-war* is anti-male. *Being assertive*—anti-female. *Interest in fixing and repairing*—

74

anti-female. *Interest in business* is anti-female. *Interest in being a professional (M.D., lawyer, etc., other than teacher)* is anti-female. The list goes on and on, and while there are areas that are considered one or the other by nearly all Western nationalities and cultures, there are some that are the specialities of particular national groups based on culture.

There are many male and female feelings involved and threatened in proscribed do's and don'ts regarding sexual practice, and I speak here of heterosexual practice. In the lower income groups, too much foreplay ending with the man in other than the man on top position is seen as a threat to his masculinity. But more about sexual muddles in the next section.

What then is male and female? For me, the answer is very simple. We have different customs and cultural habits and pressures from them, but despite them and the phony truisms therein derived—all feelings, interest, activities (other than breast nursing, etc., which man cannot do) are both male and female. This is not because we are all a little bit homosexual. It is because all these feelings are human feelings and are not naturally isolated into sexual compartments at all, except by our own learning and doing. Men and women are not born "that" different, but they may *learn* to be "that" different from each other.

Let me say that I have met homosexual men who are as "masculine" in all areas, excluding sexual preference, as it is possible to be. I have met aggressive, hard-headed, "masculine" women who are excellent sexual partners— always heterosexually—with men only. I have met "feminine" milk-toasty men whose wives had no complaint at all and who had no homosexual history or tendency whatsoever. There are people who argue that the male of the

75

species is born with a greater instinct for aggression and the female is born with a greater instinct for passivity. They point to various animals of other species as examples. (Of course, the corollary of this is that homosexuals are born homosexuals.) Well, let me say that in various species this is sometimes so and sometimes not so. The female lioness is the hunter. In Greek mythology, we see Diana, the Huntress. We still have big gaps in information about other species and their learning and communicating capacities and processes. But we are not another species. We are homo sapiens—man—and as such, we are much more than instinct-governed machines. We do learn and evaluate and, unfortunately, sometimes learn destructive ways and things. Let me point out here that—

1) I have never met a homosexual who in any way gave me the feeling that he suffered from either an inherited or congenital (from birth) illness.

2) Every homosexual that I've met (in treatment) has eventually given me ample evidence about his early family relations to demonstrate how and why he developed this symptom. Also, I have had homosexual patients (contrary to any physiological rationale) who through treatment went on to heterosexual lives. This is not easy and takes much motivation, but as in other emotional disturbances, people can grow, become healthier and get well.

So what is maleness and what is femaleness? Simply stated, this is the way I see it. Maleness is being sexually attracted to females and wanting sex with them. Femaleness is being sexually attracted to males and wanting sex with them. Feelings and interests are human and as such have no male or female connotation, unless you give them a connotation born of your own devising.

Sexual fears—frigidity and impotence

There are fears and confusions about sex which run rampant in the population and couldn't be more destructive in relating to one's self and to Max. I have found these confusions in adolescents and young adults, but also in college professors and, yes—even in doctors! They are not always apparent, because they range from the most blatantly open kind of muddlings to very subtle manifestations.

I recently saw an old man in consultation, who, after several visits, admitted to masturbating as a youth (a universal practice) but took two more sessions to state that he was always afraid that this youthful practice indicated that he might be a homosexual. This fear nagged at him (and I'm sure was destructive to him in many ways) for over fifty years, despite the fact that he could not recall any homosexual yearnings, let alone a single homosexual encounter. The fear of homosexuality is especially prevalent in men. Some analysts found this fear so prevalent, in fact, as to feel that it was universal. They reasoned that its universality was largely due to repressed or hidden actual homosexuality. They said in effect that everybody has at least some minimal homosexual impulse, which, because it is abhorred by society, is kept hidden, but that its poking up into awareness created a fear which often could not be denied. I and many other therapists do not agree with this supposition at all. I feel that there is in general much confusion and interlinking in people's minds (especially men) of success (in areas that are important to them) and sexual prowess.

Failure or relative failure in those important areas,

77

or areas in which they have invested much pride, results in feeling sexually inadequate, which means being "less of a man" and, therefore, "more of a woman,"—therefore, "maybe homosexual." So the fear of homosexuality comes up almost universally whenever a blow to one's self-esteem occurs—or a feeling of self-weakening is experienced.

I have seen men become frightened of the possibility of homosexuality when they have had business reversals or business failures; when they failed school examinations, licensing and state board examinations; when creative work was not well received critically; when a book or manuscript was turned down by a publisher. Similarly, it has occurred when men who were away from their wives masturbated for the first time in a long time; when they had great guilt over an extramarital episode, when they failed to satisfy their wives sexually, when they suffered from a short period of impotence, when they found that they were very shy in their sexual approach to girls and women.

Let us straighten out this muddle, as much as we can, here and now!

Asexuality is a very complicated and rare condition in which the individual has no sexual interest—homosexual, heterosexual, abnormal or normal. He or she simply has no sexual interest or feelings. Impotence and frigidity are symptoms of emotional difficulty and in the vast majority of cases have nothing to do with either asexuality or homosexuality. They are often related to feelings of inadequacy, greatly repressed anger, inadequate emotional maturity or development and poor sexual education and experience.

Sexual shyness is nearly always prevalent in young people and is very often seen in older people, too. It is based on inexperience, as well as feelings of inadequacy, feelings of unlovability and lack of self-acceptance, with the almost certain subsequent fear of rejection by others. It is very seldom related to any form of homosexuality whatsoever.

Homosexual fear is almost universally prevalent and as such is almost a culturally or environmentally induced phenomenon. Society, without awareness, stresses and overstresses the importance of sexuality and sexual adequacy as a prime prerequisite in self-acceptance. Sexual adequacy in turn becomes a highly complicated goal and is often interpreted in terms that are impossible to achieve. Thus sex becomes an emotionally supercharged area, and the picture is further complicated when sex becomes linked and intermeshed with many pride-invested areas in people's lives. All this rarely has anything to do with homosexuality.

Homosexuality—in which an individual desires sexual activity with a member of the same sex—is a symptom born of complicated, long-standing emotional difficulties which have been in the process of development since early childhood. As far as I'm concerned, this symptom is always linked to very disturbed familial relationships. These disturbances are manifested in the child by early confusions concerning his sexual identification. Homosexuality is a symptom of emotional disturbance. Emotional disturbance can be remedied and the homosexual can become heterosexual, but the psychotherapeutic process is long and often quite painful. It is often as difficult for the homosexual man or woman to become heterosexual as it would be for the heterosexual person to become homosexual. This means, in effect, changing the relating habits of a lifetime—no easy matter. Few homosexual people have the extraordinary motivation required to take on this great effort—but some do and are successful.

IQ—intelligence—ignorance

Intelligence quotient is an estimate of one's potential intelligence. Let me say at once that few tests have been constructed that can consistently measure this elusive characteristic with accuracy. Similarly, such tests as have been devised are useless and even destructive when used by nonexperts. They are also useless unless they are part of a large battery of tests designed to evaluate emotional functioning, including skilled interviewing. This is so because it is extremely difficult to differentiate between intellectual blocking due to emotional difficulty and to poor function due to poor intellectual endowment. Yes, emotional disturbance can temporarily prevent a person from using his thinking process effectively. I have seen children who were misdiagnosed as congenital mental defectives jump from an IQ of 60 to one of 120. Of course, these children were suffering from severe emotional disturbance.

Having a high IQ—an excellent intellectual endowment that is not blocked emotionally and that results in very high scores on IQ tests—is often confused with training, knowledge and experience. I have seen any number of intellectually gifted people who have had great difficulty in job relationships because of this confusion. Some have expected superiors to make all kinds of concessions to them on the basis of their intelligence. Others suffered from attacks of severe self-disappointment, self-rejection —and even severe self-hate, when they failed in their work, having actually been under the impression that their "smartness" would compensate for a lack of experience and knowledge. Some saw the process of learning and getting experience as demeaning and as a blow to their investment of pride in their high intelligence; thus they chronically deprived themselves of the possibility of proper training and success. Some of these people had been told from infancy about how bright they were and they actually *were* very bright. Unfortunately, they came to believe that bright people should have been "born knowing" or should in some imagined way acquire knowledge and experience without effort—thus any effort came to be looked upon as anti-intelligence or even proof of stupidity. Well, what is ignorance? It is not stupidity. It refers to the state of being ignorant and ignorant refers to the act of ignoring. Intelligence, however much in evidence, whatever the endowment, will not mitigate the ignoring of knowledge even one iota. I have met many intellectually gifted people—some with obviously extraordinary intellectual endowments—who consistently ignored knowledge, information and experience for so long that they easily fulfilled the requirements necessary to being deemed ignoramuses. I have also met people of no extraordinary intellectual endowment who, having worked hard to attain knowledge, were in no way ignorant.

This particular muddle may sound simple, even naive, trite and obvious. But not a month goes by that I don't see at least a few young people in consultation who are failing in their careers, in some part due to this "obvious" confusion. The interesting thing is that these very bright young people understand this confusion immediately—even before I finish explaining it to them. But it takes them months to appreciate its application to themselves and even more time before they can do something about the very strongly implanted feeling (and pride investment) that a high IQ precludes their being ignorant. Like all pride-invested entities, this is a difficult one to give up. It is almost impossible to give up or to combat a destructive belief, pattern or blockage that we are unaware of, but which nevertheless exerts its overwhelming effect unrelentingly.

Psychologizing and self-analyzing

Before we go further, let's get this one squared away.

By psychologizing, I mean the special kind of conversations that go on between people, in which they take each other apart piece by piece, reconstruct whole areas of their lives, make elaborate confessions and discuss psychological phenomena. Some, who are in the early stages of actual psychoanalysis, add bits and pieces from their experiences in treatment. All this goes on in a highly intellectual manner and the people who go in for this kind of activity tend to be overintellectualized. However, this is not self-analysis; it is almost never a form of communication, does not lead to self-growth and, fortunately, is often nothing more than just an exchange of elaborate words and phrases. Also it is often a form of subtle to blatant showing off. Playing analyst oneself sometimes serves as a way of getting back at one's analyst. Unfortunately, it is occasionally destructive: think of the damage an amateur surgeon could produce. Here, too, this kind of mixed group "analysis" can be used vindictively. It can open areas of one's psychological life precipitously and, in some fragile people, can prove to be quite damaging.

Self-analyzing is a very valuable process that very

few people are capable of, except after having been in psychoanalytic treatment for several years. If you can lie back (in a warm bath), relax, be open to what comes up in your mind and feelings, and can look and learn about yourself without moral judgments or recriminations, then you have a wonderful gift that can lead to much insight and growth. Unfortunately, what passes for self-analysis is often no such thing. Many people sit and think and think and think about themselves, and their thinking branches this way and that way and they continue to think about themselves and really cannot stop except with very strong distraction. This kind of "obsessive ruminating" is not at all connected to self-analysis, opening up, extending self or growth. If anything, its closer relative is psychologizing which is often an external form of obsessive ruminating. This kind of *self-thinking* is very often a subtle and sometimes a rather blatant form of self-torture. It often leads to much moralizing, breaking dictums to one's self, making all kinds of contracts and resolutions with one's self—which are soon broken and lead to self-hate. It is often used to prevent honest and valid feelings about one's self and others from entering awareness because they do not fit prescribed and acceptable standards.

Obsessive ruminating and psychologizing are sometimes rationalized as having a useful purpose under the guise of being a form of self-analysis. They are no such thing and are not even remote cousins to the analytic process. As a matter of fact, they are sometimes evidence of serious emotional disturbance and an indication that real psychoanalysis by an expert professional is necessary.

The familiar and the unfamiliar

People do not know the extent to which "clinging to the familiar" and "fear of the unfamiliar" affect their lives. This force is so prevalent in all areas of human encounter that just not knowing about it constitutes a major muddle. What am I talking about? I am saying that people will cling to the familiar, only because it is familiar, even when doing so may be highly destructive, inhibiting and even paralyzing. They would rather stick to old and bad jobs and continue to stay in long-standing destructive relationships than go on to much-improved but uncharted territory. The statement, "At least I know what I've got," is a highly significant one, but few people really know what force this clinging to the familiar plays in their lives. Knowing this—that you don't want to do something or to meet someone only because you haven't done so before, can often enable you to break a stultifying inhibition. This can help you to open the door to uncharted and enriching territory. Psychiatrists know only too well how patients stick to their neuroses, anxieties and depression, however painful, because these have become commonplace to them. For any person to meet new, really new, situations and new people, really new people, with openness and without the banner of prejudice and prejudgment often born of fear of the unfamiliar, means *taking a chance*. But this can be such an interesting, potentially rewarding chance! This cannot be done if you are unaware that you are afraid of the unfamiliar. You may not even be aware that you have narrowed your life's activities and relationships down to a minimum "safe" and repetitious pattern, which guarantees no contact with anything *outside* (unfamiliar). Or you may be aware of a tight and narrow existence but unaware of how come or what can be done about it.

It is therefore necessary to examine yourself and your recent activities and to question: Have you done anything new lately? Have you been to museums that you never before visited? Have you read books with new ideas that you never encountered before? Have you gone to places that you've never been to before or met people (and different kinds of people) that you haven't known before? Have you explored new job possibilities or the possibility of new business and cultural enterprises? If the answer is no, no and more no, then try to open up and become aware of the extent to which you cling to known territory.

Of course being in touch with your assets and having greater self-esteem and greater feeling for values and self will be enormously helpful in exploring new areas. People with little feeling for who they are rely very heavily on a known environment (and status quo—place, job, people) to give them a sense of identity. Though they do not know it and are only aware of increased anxiety—getting into new areas, especially new human encounters, often represents a potential and terrifying loss of identity. Some people cannot step out of the familiar until they have greater certainty about who they are and the solid emotional awareness that they will continue to be themselves wherever they go and whatever they do. Some people, of course, need professional help in order to accomplish this.

Contact and involvement

Involvement with things, causes, ideas and especially people is not a black and white matter. There are qualitative and quantitative differences between involvement and *involvement*.

Contact is the very briefest kind of involvement, representing what may be thought of as the most superficial and fleeting kind of touch-and-go. Yet people make contact after contact with people and activities and can't understand their lack of success. The fact is that they do not recognize the difference between a touch and an investment. And this is what involvement is all about—investment. It is more than a sustained touching or brief encounter or contact. It is the investment of one's self—yourself. This means an investment of your time, energy, and emotion. Involvement of a serious, sustained and prolonged nature seldom fails to produce at least some results. But this is no mere contact. This means sustained effort on your part and adequate prolonged caring enough about—so as to give an ample measure of yourself. Of course, no amount of flitting from one "contact" to another can equal a single prolonged, let alone profound, involvement as regards either a person or activity.

Dependency and sick dependency

This is a muddle that is often fed by the unrealistic all or none, black and white approach to life. So let's get this straight—all healthy human beings are dependent. As children they are dependent on adults for their well-being. Unlike other animals, human beings are born helpless and, in many ways, incomplete. But people are dependent on people all of their lives, however much they "grow up." We are community creatures and our emotional well-being depends on our ability to communicate and to relate to our fellows. We do not do well when we are emotionally or even physically isolated. Long periods of physical isolation (shipwrecked people on life rafts and in experimental isolation studies) soon produce hallucinations—an effort to conjure up people whom we so desperately need. It seems that just as tissues need oxygen, our psychic processes need people with whom to be in *contact* and with whom to be involved. Of course, we also need and depend on each other in the exchange of mutual goods and services. The more complex and intricate our society becomes, the more dependent we become on the skills of others.

Many people confuse healthy human interdependency with sick dependency and have the notion that they ought to strive for the ability to function completely alone. Since this cannot be done, they become disappointed with themselves and see themselves as sickly, dependent and inadequate people.

Well, chances are that just about all of us are dependent in a sick way, too. However, the extent of our sick or neurotic or morbid dependency, as some workers call it, is all-important. What is sick dependency in contrast to *normal dependency?*

First, let me say that most people are not consciously aware of their sick dependency. It taints and sometimes governs nearly every aspect of their lives without consciousness on their part. This is not too different from long-standing chronic physical illnesses, in which symptoms of the illness have become a totally "familiar" way of life and the sick individual has no awareness of being sick at all. To a large degree, sick dependency is a carry-over from the normal dependency of childhood. It is as if the adult had not grown up, or evolved out from his early dependent years. He is still dependent on an almost childish level, but he has transferred his early dependency on others for his "real" physical needs to dependency on others for "unrealistic" emotional needs. In sick dependency, he functions as a person who has lost touch with or never has had a sense of, individual self or identity. He is not in touch with his values and really does not have a solid feel of who he is. He needs other people, and especially another person, to lean on, to give him a sense of wholeness, and to constantly reassure him by means of approval, affection and admiration so that he can function. It is as if control of his own life and the freedom of choice in any of his life's activities are not contained within himself but have passed on to how other people feel. Of course this kind of dependency makes one tremendously and unrealistically—that is, disproportionately and inappropriately—concerned with other people's opinions. Since his identity is out there with other people, he can hardly make a move without adequate consultation, reassurance, and extreme concern with how they will feel about it. This kind of person will feel completely alone when he is by himself since being in his own company feels like being in the company of nobody. Thus he will be terrified of solitude and will feel loneliness and homesickness as crushing burdens. Lengthy or permanent removal of the person or people he has come to count on as part of his emotional constellation can result in severe anxiety, depression and even suicide. Without other people he feels emotionally dead and physical death seems to him like an almost natural next step.

People suffering from intense "sick dependency" will be very much concerned with and confused about love. Love from others and especially *someone* will be as important as oxygen is to all people. To these people, love really means a gratification of their dependency needs. This love is not at all related to mutual give-and-take, concern and responsibility. This love is rather concerned with show me, tell me, give me, reassure me, do for me.

It is small wonder that people who have had prolonged contact with very dependent people feel "sucked dry" and "emptied." Of course, this kind of "love" is bound to bring bitter disappointment and bitterness. Nobody can gratify the infantile yearnings of an adult. When the dependent person is thwarted in his needs, he often reacts with great rage. *But* since anger may alienate the person or people he continues to need, he represses his rage, convincing himself that he is not angry and his anger then takes the form of anxiety and depression. Thus, in many "adults" attacks of anxiety and depression are really the equivalent of infantile temper tantrums. "Suicide" is often the equivalent of a major temper tantrum, designed to get even with the person who thwarted the dependent person. These severe reactions may sound strange, and on realistic adult grounds they are strange and inappropriate. But, considering the severity of the degree of need in an individual who alone feels completely empty and "like nobody," these reactions are perfectly logical.

Karen Horney in her various works describes this kind of individual in detail. May I say here that Dr. Horney's brilliance as an anatomist of neurotic human character structure and personality has never been excelled.

Independence

This much-extolled virtue is constantly confused with some pretty sick stuff. I am all for mature, individualistic, self-igniting, spontaneous decisions and actions based on being really in touch with one's self, one's feelings and one's values, and based on the mature ability and willingness to take full responsibility for one's life.

However, there are many people to whom independence becomes a godlike cult to be worshipped above all other things, a kind of fetish and even a way of life. All these people are using "independence" as a rationalization for some pretty compulsive stuff. These people are not independent nor do they really strive for independence. The really independent person likes people, likes to be with people, likes to and can work with and trust people. He can do so because he is not afraid of hidden and powerful dependency feelings and he is not afraid of being taken over, swamped, absorbed. His individual identity is not in jeopardy because he always has a solid feel of himself in relation to himself and to other people and in familiar and unfamiliar places and situations. The "independence fetishist," on the other hand, uses a so-called quest for independence to cover up a profound fear of strong, repressed dependency needs and a great fear of people and involvement with them. These people do not have a choice in the matter—they *must* keep their emotional distance from other people. Closeness becomes a great threat to freedom and feels like "being choked" or "being drained," and is extremely anxiety-provoking. Since many of these people are also very dependent people, they are caught in the dilemma of a terrible need for people and, simultaneously, a terrible fear of people. They attempt to resolve this dilemma by having short-term noninvolved relationships which satisfy their dependent needs without the threat of real emotional closeness.

In these people, threat of a sustained contractual agreement of any kind can, of course, produce severe anxiety. Again and again I see patients who have made much of independence go into a serious panic just before marriage, just before signing a long term-contract and at the time of nearly any written agreement.

You can readily see how destructive this kind of bogus independence can be in relating to Max, on any level, especially when one does not know that he is functioning this way at all. Due to our own cultural pre-occupation with "being independent," these people are often mistakenly seen as reserved, strong, silent, profound thinkers who must be listened to with great seriousness with each descent from Olympus. This, of course, strengthens the victim's feeling that nothing is wrong with him and is a further deterrent to awareness of a very serious problem.

Health/sickness

There are people who, at the slightest sign of sickness, feel that they are in a state of complete collapse and well on their way to the cemetery. This comes of many things, including great feelings of fragility and a huge (usually buried and hidden) fund of hopelessness and pessimism. But confusion about health and sickness also plays a role.

When an individual has a sore throat and says, "I'm sick," he is, in fact, telling the truth. Not only is his throat, a part of himself, sick, but it may also affect his feeling about himself generally, so that he feels a general malaise or sickness. But how about the vast majority of his physical being which is not sick, which is, in fact, healthy? Our language ideas are so designed that a person calls himself sick when a single symptom or evidence of sickness is apparent. Yet he does not call himself sick and says that he is healthy when they are not present or apparent. Is there a state of health or a state of sickness? I speak here of emotional as well as physical health. There certainly are states of relative health, relative well-being, relative comfort and relatively good ability to function. There certainly are states of relative discomfort and disability or inability to function. Absolute sickness and absolute health do not exist. The only absolute I know of is death. The state of death still remains absolute and complete (although researchers are at work on changing this!).

Health and sickness are static, absolute-sounding words that poorly describe what actually goes on. These *words* do not adequately describe the flux, flow and changeability of the human process of living and dying.

However, these words and others are the only ones we have, so we must make the best of them. But in so doing let's not get caught in word traps. Let us try to keep our conceptions of important forces in our lives as clear and precise as we can, so that we are not victimized by muddled and confusing concepts.

Health and sickness are not mutually exclusive. They are part and parcel of the same process—*living*—and go on, hand in hand, so well integrated that it is often impossible to separate them. When we separate them we do so in order to better understand and to be better able to help ourselves. In so doing, however, we often feed the fiction that they are separate, exclusive, and absolute entities—all not true! From the second of conception, through birth and until death, the individual in question will be living and will be healthy and sick. There will be aspects of himself (physical and emotional) that will be constructive and self- and life-affirming, and other aspects that will be destructive and life-rejecting. The healthiest people will also have sick aspects and the sickest will have healthy aspects.

People who are relatively healthy can, to a larger extent, tap the assets they have, but their asset supply may be very limited or even small. There are people who can hardly function at all, let alone tap their resources or integrate their assets, but who have an enormous fund of assets and, therefore, much potential brilliant functioning ability. Of course, the ratio of assets—healthy function and sick or destructive function—is all-important in how successful a person will be in relating to Max. But this is an extraordinarily complicated and misunderstood issue, which is grossly confused by the vast oversimplifications of concepts of absolute health and sickness. Psychiatrists have to be intimately acquainted with the juxtaposition of these forces in order to determine prognosis, goals and

93

how fast or slow the treatment ought to go. Great success in business or as a sportsman does not preclude the possibility of great fragility, rigidity, and even impending psychiatric disaster.

Why does this concern us now? Because it is important to realize that although you may be feeling sick, you may be quite healthy, and similarly, you may be feeling well and be quite sick. It is important to realize that a symptom does not mean sickness exclusively. It points to a problem, a situation—so don't, if you can help it, look upon a symptom as a whole. When a person is depressed or very anxious, it is most difficult to realize that the anxiety and depression are symptoms. They are not the whole person and *do not* constitute all the forces playing a role in his life. At the time of depression, he feels that all there is in life and in this world are depressed black days. But it is not true. However depressed an individual may be, there is much, much, much going on in him and much of it is in the service of constructive life-affirming goals. It can be very valuable to at least have some understanding of the realistic health/sickness interplay in order to take a good look at one's self and also to mitigate hopelessness.

Break down and break up

People often say, "I had a nervous breakdown" or "My nerves are shot" or "I have bad nerves," etc. Let's get this one ironed out. When people have a so-called nervous breakdown, they are actually referring to a breakdown of function, that is, a temporary inability or great difficulty in doing what they ordinarily can do because of one or another kind of emotional symptomology (depression, anxiety, etc.). Nervous breakdown, nervous exhaustion, etc., are a very poor choice of words because no such thing has happened. There have been no changes in the nervous system, no deterioration, no wearing out, weakening, breaking down or anything else of the sort. As a matter of fact, organic diseases of the nervous system (inflamed nerves, multiple sclerosis, brain tumors, etc.) almost always manifest themselves in entirely different ways.

I have never seen a so-called nervous breakdown caused by any physical entity, and that includes overwork and fatigue. I have seen people who have, as a result of great emotional upset, been unable to sleep and thus have become exhausted. I have also seen people who, because of emotional difficulties, have overworked—but *not* the reverse. What, then, is the cause of neurotic emotional upsets, reactions or upheavals that sometimes prevent an individual from carrying on life as usual? (I do not include severe mental illness here.) In almost all cases, I feel that what is involved is a tremendous blow to one's pride in one or another area. This can be a marriage failure, business reversal, examination failure, etc. In any case, it is a blow to one's concept of what one has thought himself to be and as a result has unleashed much self-hate and self-doubt which is converted to anxiety and depression. The exact process of how this happens and the particular kind of reaction will vary with the individual. Of course, much will depend on the person's past life and his ways of relating to himself and to others.

To understand this whole process in depth requires much theoretical study and training as well as intimate knowledge of the person in question. I only touch upon this to indicate to you that there is no breakdown in anything but immediate function. I prefer, as my own analyst did, to call these reactions break-ups. Break-up is a more realistic term because what is really happening during a great emotional upheaval is a break-up of old, learned and often rigid neurotic patterns. This break-up results in great pain in the form of anxiety and depression, but many people cannot grow or change markedly without the break-up of old ways and without ensuing growing pains. This may sound peculiar, but many people who will never have a break-up or any symptoms of emotional disturbance are in our (deeper psychoanalytic) terms, sicker people than those who do! They are sicker because they are more rigid, cannot let go and cannot permit a break-up to take place so that reevaluation and growth can follow. The individual who can let go, who *must* let go (due to hurt pride, etc.), is often demonstrating sufficient flexibility to allow for a healthier reassemblage to take place. In view of this, the statement "One must get sicker before one gets better" is almost always true. I say *almost* because I would change it to "The ability to feel the pain of a break-up of old patterns is often evidence of the possibility of letting go of them and establishing new, healthier ways of life."

"There is only one right choice or decision"

Again and again, I see people tear themselves apart because they actually believe this statement. Actually, in the vast majority of situations there are any number of "right" or "good" possible choices and decisions that would work out well. This is what more often than not causes the difficulty. If there were only one correct choice or decision, there would be relatively little difficulty. The right or only decision would be made and that would be the end (and the beginning) of a happy story. However, since there are almost always many right choices (or at least more than one), it requires making a stand and taking responsibility and getting involved in choosing one of the several equally good ones. If one is mature, knows who he is and is willing to stand up for himself and whatever and whichever way he chooses, fully aware of the multiplicity of possibilities, then it's easy. But if a person is unwilling to commit himself to a decision and, on top of it, believes that only one decision will do—then he is in conflict and troubled indeed.

I particularly recall a young man I was seeing in treatment who was very intelligent, talented and had many assets. *But* he was quite immature, frightened of serious, prolonged involvement, and really felt incapable of taking responsibility for a decision. For years he went with any number of girls, always looking for the "right girl," and, for years, he flitted from one career to the other, unable to decide which was the "right one." Nearly all of the girls he went out with were fine, attractive, bright young women with whom it would have been possible for him to have had a sustained and deep relationship. With his considerable talent he could easily have been successful at any of the careers he was constantly contemplating. In actuality, no one decision was better than another and any one of the possible decisions would have been a good and right one. However, in order to make this decision, he had to get over his feeling of inadequacy, tap his resources and grow up emotionally in many ways. He also had to come to the realization that there were in fact a large number of "right" choices—jobs, girls—but that he would have to take responsibility for that choice. In so doing, he also had to be willing to give up other "right choices" because he could not be all things at the same time. Most difficult of all, of course, he had to eventually take the chance of getting seriously involved. He was able to do this, but it took much work, time and motivation.

So the existence of choice, and it nearly always exists, can be used as an excuse for not making any choice and can be felt as an awful burden. It can throw a person into constant conflict, confusion and anxiety.

Please remember, knowing that a choice of several good moves exists can give the freedom to take responsibility for a decision and for living one's own life as one chooses.

Thoughts—feelings—actions

Thoughts, feelings, and actions, though they may have a common thread, are not the same thing, do not have the same effect on you or Max or the general environment in which you live. This sounds so logical and obvious as to be axiomatic, but you'd be surprised how many people (with little or no awareness) lump them all together as one and then go on to judge themselves accordingly. This, of course, makes them frightened to feel, frightened to think and often results in a modified form of the very action in which they do not wish to participate. Let's destroy this particularly destructive muddle.

If thought, feeling and action were one and the same thing, there would indeed be considerable chaos in the streets. All kinds of strange things would be happening constantly. Cars would smash into crowds of people, fires would be set, obscenities would be shouted, parks would become huge bathrooms, people would be slowly tortured on the streets, sexual activity would be open and rampant and much of it would be "different" than that experienced in most bedrooms of the country. Yes, a certain amount of this goes on anyway, but it would all seem like child's play compared with what would happen if all thoughts and feelings were directly translated into actions.

The fact is that people feel, and they think and they decide how and if to act and not to act. A man may have a feeling or an urge to run over to a pretty girl on the street and squeeze her breast. But if he is relatively healthy, he thinks about this, knows that this is taboo in our society (and would be destructive to him), decides not to do it and walks on. Thus, the feeling and thought have not been translated into action and the girl in question remains completely intact, usually unaware of the urge, feeling, thinking and decision she precipitated.

We all have some very "peculiar thoughts" from time to time. This is especially so when we are anxious or very tired or just before we go to sleep or just on awakening. That is when our guard is down. Some of them are so grotesque, out of context, appearing suddenly and without apparent rhyme or reason, that they resemble the strangest kinds of nightmares and make us very anxious. No—they're not signs or evidence of insanity. If this were so, we would all be quite insane. That we are aware of their "peculiar" nature and aware that they are out of keeping with "all the rest" that goes on in us is indication of very good judgment and a strong connection to reality. Some very disturbed (seriously ill) people cannot make this differentiation. To them, these thoughts seem like any others and are not peculiar at all.

Well, where do peculiar thoughts come from? They come from feelings that we repress, which we don't like, largely because they don't fit in with our concept of what we think we ought to feel and whom we think we ought to be. But we also repress these feelings because we see them as actions and pass judgment on them as if they were actions—which, of course, they are not.

The stronger a feeling is, the more it is repressed, the more grotesque the shape of it will be when it finally comes through as a thought. Thus, a small feeling of anger toward someone, repressed again and again, can eventually snowball and come through quite distorted and unrecognizable. A sudden picture popping into one's head of a friend's head rolling in the gutter may originally have been a simple "You irritate me." Obviously, people who have great difficulty expressing their feelings to themselves and others may be subject to strange thoughts. But these thoughts are almost never translated into action (when they are, we are dealing with a different condition entirely) and disappear when the individual learns to accept and to express feelings. (I'll discuss "peculiar thoughts" at greater length later.)

Knowing that feelings, thoughts and actions are not the same is very important. This is so because it frees you to feel what you will, think what you will and act according to decisions you make as you will. Thus, you will not cut off feelings and thoughts which you are afraid of because they are inappropriate. You will be better able to let what you feel make itself apparent to you, so that you are in touch with all parts of you and able to use all parts of you in relating to Max. Since a feeling does not affect anyone unless it becomes an action, let it come and let it be a part of you so that you can think and decide freely. Remember that feelings *will* affect someone—namely you—if they are bottled up, held down and become potentially explosive in the forms of anxiety, depression and psychosomatic illness.

If you have a "peculiar" thought, remember that it is

not an action—it has hurt nobody. Don't shove it out of the way. Take a look and try to trace its origin. You may be able to find the feeling it came from. This will extend your cognition of yourself, in the feeling department, so that there will be much more of you to relate to Max with as a winner. My own analyst used to say that when a mother has the thought "Drop dead" regarding her child, it means drop dead *but only* for a little while, because all that she really feels is "I'm tired and irritated and would like a vacation from motherhood for just a little while."

Judge, jury and executioner

Are you one of the many people who, without awareness, function as judge, jury and executioner with both yourself and others? Some of the common manifestations of this muddle are not allowing yourself a good time or satisfaction in things, chastising yourself, being irritated with yourself, moodiness, depression and being frequently irritated with friends, annoyed by them, cutting them off so that your social circle is getting smaller and smaller.

I have many patients who, without awareness, for years have functioned as the judge, jury, executioner trinity. They apply this judgment to themselves as well as to others. In this kind of court, the jury is seldom out for more than a few seconds, because the judge is not interested in evidence as much as he is in judgment and execution—both of which are invariably and inappropriately harsh. In the individual himself, any imperfection, failure to live up to an expected role, hurt pride or unwanted feeling is seen as a major crime. The sentence is usually depression with anxiety and self-beating in the form of undue aggravation, worrying and self-degradation ("you are no good," repeated many, many times). Where Max is concerned, the court is usually more lenient, but it's still a hanging jury. Max commits a crime in the form of a slight—hurting the court's pride, lack of a proper invitation or a reciprocal gift—some one of innumerable possibilities. Max is not told of his crime. He is not permitted to plead his case. Evidence is never presented. But, mercifully, the judgment and execution of same are relatively gentle. Max is simply banished from the world of the court and is never to be contacted again. This gentle judgment can readily be understood when you realize that Max is only Max, and one must not expect as much from Max as one does from the court (oneself). Besides, you can get rid of Max—but how can you get rid of yourself?

In any case, it is very difficult, if not impossible, to be open and accepting of others' foibles, let alone to effect winning relationships with them, if you apply only self-hate, harsh judgments and painful execution on yourself, with little or no mitigating self-acceptance.

Psyche and soma and thinking and feeling

The mind (thinking processes) and physical processes and feelings or emotions all take place in one human being (with due respect to mystic and religious concepts of soul), in one body—one physical being. This is obvious and there's nothing very original or profound about the statement. But so many people who "understand" this statement and agree with it entirely, don't agree with it at all, on a little deeper level. They really feel differently and act accordingly. They function in a compartmentalized way, so that it seems that they are really several people rather than one. These people have split themselves into a psyche (mind) and soma (body) dichotomy and often a thinking and feeling dichotomy, too. For any one person to relate to Max successfully is complicated enough. But for one person who operates like two or three or more persons to relate to Max on a successful level becomes extraordinarily difficult.

Thoughts spring from feelings and feelings from thoughts and all of it is affected and stimulated in countless ways by the environment and particularly by relationships to outside people. All of it is made possible by a living, functioning body which provides the necessary chemistry, and whose chemistry is, in turn, constantly affected by, changed by, and adapted to the very feelings and thoughts it makes possible.

An interesting corollary of the above is that all illness is psychosomatic. How can an illness exist without a soma (body)? How can an illness exist without emotional repercussions? How can emotional repercussions exist without again affecting the body (glandular secretions, etc.)? How can emotional upsets exist without affecting Max and vice versa? Of course, they can't. They must all go on at once, as a cycle or continuum.

There is a muddle within a muddle in that many people confuse hypochondria with psychosomatic illness. Hypochondriacs suffer from imagined illnesses. Their illness consists of the fear and delusion that they have illnesses which, in fact, do not exist. Psychosomatic illnesses are very real. They refer to a group of illnesses that seem to be particularly affected by the patient's emotions—that is, much more so than other physical illnesses. In these illnesses, the physiological disability is not imagined. It is very real, indeed, and often can be seen or demonstrated very readily by X-ray, laboratory tests, etc. Some of these are duodenal ulcer, bronchial asthma and various skin eruptions, and they are all very real.

"I don't believe in psychiatry"

This is a statement I hear again and again, sometimes made by seemingly knowledgeable, sophisticated, intelligent, well-informed people. Told to people who are suffering from some emotional disability, and who are consequently often very suggestable and in desperate need of professional help, this statement can be very damaging indeed.

What do these people mean? Taken literally the statement makes no sense at all. Does it mean that they don't believe that mental illness or emotional disturbances exist? Do they believe that mental illness is just a question of willpower—"Make up your mind and get well" or "Don't pay attention to it; just do what you have to." If this were so, we could happily empty our many overcrowded state hospitals. I've yet to meet a person suffering from emotional illness who does not (deep down) want to get well. Do they mean that they don't believe a specialty concerning itself with the emotional ills ought to exist—another way of saying that people suffering from emotional ills are hopeless, so why bother? Do they mean that anybody—let's say illiterate people—untrained to do anything else, ought to care for the mentally ill—sort of a return to the Middle Ages? All these meanings are possible. But the several times I've had the opportunity to get to know the people who make these statements, I found that they had one thing in common. They were all inordinately afraid of going crazy. They are afraid of finding out about themselves, convinced that that which is hidden must all be bad. In truth, they feel quite hopeless about themselves. In believing that they don't believe in psychiatry, they are in a magical and irrational way fending off the possibility of craziness in themselves.

This would be much the same as a woman who has doubts about her ability to conceive and to give birth normally and without damage to herself saying, "I don't believe in obstetrics." This is also similar to the individual who avoids doctors in order to avoid sickness. When some of these people finally go to the doctor they are angry if he finds nothing wrong (a waste of money) and angry if he finds that something is wrong. They then feel that they would not have known if they didn't go and if they didn't know then, in effect, they wouldn't be sick. The irrational logic continues then to the conclusion that doctors cause illnesses, so stay away from them.

This kind of denial of reality by avoidance is very common and takes many forms. As I said earlier, the fear of madness is particularly powerful and prevalent and so is the statement, "I don't believe in psychiatry." This, then, is an attempt to obliterate an entire area of great fear—sweep it all under the carpet.

To further complicate the matter, the statement and attempt at belief do not work. The fear is not allayed for very long, since the cause and roots of the fear go on intact. To further cope with the situation, the very individual who doesn't "believe in psychiatry" is usually preoccupied with it. He is always discussing, analyzing, criticizing, psychologizing and fostering all kinds of confusions. He is very adamant (not unusual wherever there is a complete lack of expertise) about any further unsuccessful attempts to allay his anxiety.

Of course there are other statements made along the way—often blatant projections of what the individual himself is really feeling—and these can be quite revealing. Some of them are: "Psychiatrists are all a little crazy" (even though this person may never have met a psychiatrist). "Psychiatrists make more money than all other doctors" (not true, they are very low on the medical economic ladder). "Psychiatrists' children have the biggest problems." "If you get psychiatric treatment, you will get a divorce." "If you get psychiatric treatment, you will lose your talent." "If you get psychiatric treatment, you will hate your mother, father and wife or husband." "Psychiatrists will turn you against God and religion." "Psychiatric treatment results in sexual promiscuity." "All psychiatrists are Jewish." "Psychiatrists are Communists." "Doctors become psychiatrists because they can't stand the sight of blood." "Doctors who are physically ill become psychiatrists because it is less demanding." "They can read your mind." "You come away brainwashed, made over in their image and having to give up your own values and beliefs." "I know people who have been going for years and who are still exactly the same." "He used to be a nice guy—did everything for everybody and now just cares about himself."

These statements go on and on and some get quite irrational in an attempt to repress one's own fear of insanity—and being "found out." Then, too, there is much that goes on in movies, TV, and in the patter of comedians that extends these irrational beliefs and fosters a disdain and contempt for the emotionally disturbed and those concerned with helping them.

I would like to close this muddled issue with just one

more observation, a corollary to the above. It is very interesting to psychiatrists and particularly to those trained in psychoanalysis (at least fifteen years of intensive study and training) that lay people almost never discuss the technical aspects of any medical specialty. Can you remember a discussion of cardiac surgery or neurosurgery or dermatology or pathology or internal medicine or even the technical aspects of obstetrics? I doubt it. Well, the one exception is psychiatry. Here, there is no hesitancy whatsoever. This is particularly true of psychoanalysis where there are so many "experts." In this specialty, above all—the one requiring the most technical and complicated training and time—"expert" opinions, discussions and advice abound. Much of this comes from half-truths and is motivated solely by unresolved problems. Unfortunately, the effects are not always innocuous and innocent. They can be quite damaging and destructive to the impressionable and suggestible.

"He loved me"—fixations or crushes—and love

For years now, I have seen a great number of marriages mainly motivated and based on the statement, "He loved me."

It usually is the woman who comes to consult me. I say, "Jane, you state that you and your husband have nothing particularly in common. You come from different backgrounds, different age groups and have different interests. You say that you never found him "that" attractive physically. Did you know all this then?"

"No, I never thought about it at all."

107

"Did you feel that you loved him?"

"No."

"Then, what do you think motivated you? I mean, why did you marry him? Was it because you felt it was expected of you—the thing to do? Was it because you wanted to leave your parents' home and couldn't do it alone?"

"No, it was none of those things."

"Then, what?"

"He loved me."

"He loved you?"

"Yes, he kept telling me how much he loved me."

"How did you feel about him?"

"I don't really know. I guess I thought I loved him— he kept saying he loved me. I never got so much attention in my life. Funny."

"What is?"

"How now we can't stand the sight of each other."

Jane is not talking about love or about any of the things that make a sustained relationship, let alone a marriage, possible. She is saying in effect that she was overwhelmed and terribly impressed by the fact that somebody could apparently "love" her. Most of the "Janes" that I've met were very immature, inadequate, emotionally undeveloped people. They were people who had very shaky concepts of who they were, what they stood for and where they were going. They were people with very poor self-esteem and they felt completely unlovable. They were also sick, dependent people. That anybody could profess strong feeling (here called love) for them and interest in them is felt as a one-in-a-million miracle— a fantastic, beautiful dream come true. This is confused with *love* and is seen as a panacea for all the accumulated problems, ills and hurts of the past. All this has nothing whatsoever to do with mature love. Since this kind of relationship cannot possibly fulfill the multitude of neurotic needs (e.g., dependency), let alone healthy needs, the "marriage" usually remains static for a while. As the impossible demands for reassurance grow, it then deteriorates very rapidly, leaving both people confused and hurt.

"But, doctor, he loved me so" has much in common with fixations and crushes which too often also pass for love. Here, too, we see one-sided, unilateral affairs, which have nothing whatsoever to do with emotional concern, responsibility or give-and-take between two people. Crushes are part of the normal development of children and they are particularly evident in adolescents. However, this can be disastrous when confused with love by "adults" and when attempts are made to translate this kind of reaction to love and marriage. The crush or fixation is usually a completely one-way street—with worship at a distance and little real "knowing" of each other, let alone emotional exchanging taking place.

The crush or fixation is usually based on one or another idealization, which is projected or displaced to the worshipped person. Thus, John may have a crush on Jane because Jane represents his sexual ideal (all that he has learned and been conditioned to seek and to respond to in a sexual partner); his mother for whom he has undue and unresolved yearnings; a girl he knew as a child who talked or looked or walked like Jane and of whom he has dreamed for years; a projection of his own idealizations —that is, of all the things he would like to be and which he has convinced himself she is; a composite of all the "ideal characteristics" that he thinks his woman ought to have.

During the period of the fixation, nothing and nobody can convince John to just take a look, to see, to listen, to get to know Jane. He is in the grip of a powerful obsession and is convinced that he *does* "know" her. This obsessive belief is based on his enormous need to believe that he has finally found the fulfillment of his years of yearnings (based on projected needs of which he is totally unaware). No logical rationale will move him. Yet he hardly knows Jane, the real person, at all. He only knows Jane—the screen—upon which he projects a composite image with which he is obsessed. Of course Jane falls short of his expectations, which are usually inordinately exorbitant, making the crush possible in the first place. His expectations are further frustrated because Jane and his ideals have only a one-in-a-million chance of being even remotely connected.

Strangely (or not so strangely when we consider the number of immature people who live mainly in their imaginations), the Johns and Janes abound. Not only that —they go on for years, fooling themselves and people around them into believing that the "he loves me" and "crush phenomenon" are manifestations of "love." Following this kind of muddle we hear statements like—"They were such a nice couple, so much in love. Can't understand why their marriage broke up."

Well, what about love—mature, adult love? This can be and has been the subject of volumes and volumes of words. I want to contribute just enough of my own here in an attempt to clear up this all-important muddle—one that couldn't be more destructive to marriage and family.

Love, real love, between two fairly well-developed (emotionally) people (adults) is never at a distance, is never a one-way street, and is never a purely sexual experience to the exclusion of all else. A sexual encounter exclusive of all else can be most satisfying in many ways —but isn't love. Love, measured in terms of sexual excitation and number of orgasms is an extremely naïve and primitive interpretation of the most complicated and meaningful of human encounters.

110

In order for two people to love each other (to be "in love") and through sex to "make love" (much more than mutual sexual satiation, and people *in* love can *make* love with and without satiation and orgasms), they must *know* each other. I speak here, again, of knowing in the deepest sense of knowing. This kind of knowing does not come in a flash or without work. Sexual feelings and attraction can be there in a "flash" and this is fine—if you don't mistake it for love.

In order to love, considerable relating must take place. Relationships are not things that are suddenly or simply "there" in full bloom. I am all for the chemistry that takes place between two people. I believe in it, even though I don't really know much about it. There *is* a "certain something"—a very important something—that happens to certain couples and not others. I don't believe it can be manufactured, and without it, the strong, deep, wonderful feelings for each other won't be there. *But* it sometimes does not reveal itself until some time has passed and even when it does, it is not enough. You still need to relate; the relating—the give-and-take, the exchange of ideas, feelings, mutual interests and interest in each other as well as the emotional investment in each other and the growing together with each other (increasingly as a single unit) vis-à-vis other people and the world—is absolutely indispensable. It is crucial. There is no substitute.

This relating (I prefer to use the word relating rather than relationship—relationship has a static, complete connotation while relating sounds more like the real thing—the ever-growing, ever-changing process between two people) isn't just there. It takes time and it takes energy and it means that two people have to be together in various activities (including solitude) as well as social situations with other people. Occasional dates on weekends

111

largely spent in darkened theaters or noisy nightclubs and restaurants do not contribute to knowing each other deeply or to relating. Dating, sexual activity (petting and intercourse) can actually go on for months—even years— with little or no communication taking place. (This can happen with or without words. Words are often small talk and little else.) I feel that an unparalleled opportunity to get to know each other is offered when young people go to school together. They can spend many hours in each other's company engaged in mutual work, motivated by common goals, in a natural and uncontrived situation.

What are the basic ingredients that permit people to get to really know each other, to relate on a sustained basis and to love? Sexual attraction and sustained sexual interest are extremely important. In order to be mutually attracted to each other, both partners must first have a capacity for sexual excitation and interest, that is, they must have at least some of the sexual assets described earlier and discussed at greater length in the next section. They must also be willing to read and to educate themselves and to explore and to grow in their sexual knowledge of each other in an effort to be happy and to give sexual happiness. Sustained successful sexual activity is not just there. It is "there" only if both partners work at it, develop it and are willing to be constantly creative so that it doesn't become dull, routine and boring.

Will sex be the chemistry? Yes. It will provide the spark and also the means to express closeness and love. In a way, sex represents the beginning or Part I. Now, what about Part II, or the middle? This consists of all things, interests, activities, goals shared in common. But this is immediately handicapped if people are too disparate in age, energy levels, language, cultural characteristics, customs, interests, etc. I am not saying that two people ought to be carbon copies of each other. It is infinitely more interesting and rewarding if each brings his or her own unique, individual spark born of being a person in his or her own right as well as having had different experiences. But I do also speak of common frames of reference. It is much easier for people to communicate if they are born of the same generation, have similar customs and language, have similar levels of intellectual endowment, have similar educational backgrounds, have similar interests and sources of enjoyment, and have similar levels of emotional maturity. This common frame of reference will make it much more possible for them to communicate with each other meaningfully. With disparate frames of reference, people can communicate and relate, but they must have very powerful and sustained motivation as well as great flexibility and considerable ability to learn.

Part III, the end product, the most creative aspect of a mature sexual relationship and, therefore, really another beginning, too, are children. Children will convert a relationship into a family. They will be the most powerful and sustained objects of interest. Potentially, they will be the strongest glue of all, representing the most creative aspect of the fusion of two people.

Mature people in love want children, not only as links to the future, or because of a love for all children, but as a creative expression and manifestation of their relationship. Children are born of their love for each other and continue to represent their love for each other. Therefore, people maturely in love must love their children who, in a wonderful cycle, go on reminding them of their creative love for each other.

When a young man says, "I love her," does he mean love or a crush? If the "love" is not reciprocal, then it is a crush. It is basic to love that it be reciprocal—flowing up and back between the people who are loving or in love. These people like to be together, in and out of bed.

113

These people have been relating, intensively, for a prolonged period of time. These people "care" about each other and each other's happiness. They care about themselves, but they care and feel responsible for each other even more than they do about themselves. These people are more concerned about loving than about being loved.

I had a patient who sincerely believed that he "loved" a different girl every six months. The same patient sincerely thought that he had a "nervous breakdown" at the end of each affair. He actually became slightly depressed with each parting (which, for a long time, he was unwilling to admit that he himself instigated). He was not in love nor did he have a nervous breakdown. He just had a very superficial emotional experience. It was a long time before he had the capacity to love. He first had to have a "self" to love with, as well as sufficient emotional development, feelings and contact with his feelings.

The love I speak of must take place between two people of the opposite sex and will directly depend on what they bring to the loving experience. I can't imagine being a "little in love" or "loving a little," any more than I can conceive of a woman being a little pregnant.

In love, the relating that takes place is never static. It is a constantly growing, merging, creative process between two people.

But, for this stuff "that makes the world go round," we need two people who have considerable maturity, health, assets and seeds of health, and a real desire to share, to care, to give and to take in an ever-flowing emotional exchange.

Responsibility, guilt, blame, fault, punishment

This is a very common muddle and one that prevents growing up, often contributing to sustaining immaturity for a lifetime. It is destructive to Max, whoever he is—child, wife, husband, teacher, student, boss, etc. It often goes something like this: "All right, I'm feeling guilty enough so don't tell me any more." There are more subtle manifestations, too: "Why am I tired? After I found out what I did, I beat myself over the head all night." "I'll tell you, I feel so guilty, I could die." "OK, chew me out, tell me off, I mean really tell me off." "Why do you remind me? You trying to make me feel guilty or something? I feel bad enough. What else should I do, should I tear myself apart?"

The saddest part of all this is that while these people may very well feel a real sense of guilt, blame, fault and a desire for punishment, they honestly think that they are in the process of taking mature responsibility for a decision or action. Well, nothing could be further from the truth. The fact is that they are being extremely infantile, and I don't say this in a judgmental way. I am being purely clinical because, in effect, they have not moved very far (if at all) from the infantile position of reward and punishment as deserved. As children they said, in effect or in actuality, "I'm sorry, I shouldn't have done it. I don't want to get hit, so I won't do it anymore." As "adults" the same thing is going on except that the punishment is now inflicted by oneself—usually in the form of worry, self-chastisement, degradation, depression and self-deprivation.

I once had a patient whose mother deprived her of

115

something she liked ("no movies for a month") when she did something wrong. As an adult "doing something wrong" was always followed by statements like, "I'm no damn good," "I really don't deserve him" (her husband), "They ought to take everything and everybody away from me." She would also get seriously depressed, sometimes to the point of nonfunctioning. This depression was always preceded by losing a particular item she valued most—a watch, a new dress, a purse, etc. But the guilt and the punishment, in the form of depression and deprivation (losing things), changed nothing at all. It resulted in no increased understanding or insight. It added nothing to her maturity, to her ability to stand up for herself and to decide whether she wanted to change (vis-à-vis her husband) or not. It did not give her one iota more of self or of values or anything else of merit. Unlike its effect in her childhood, guilt-punishment did not deter her from again doing what she thought was wrong. Actually, it made her do what was "wrong" more often, in a peculiar attempt to allay the suffering that came from her guilt and self-hating punishment. Thus, her guilt was a very destructive emotion, which often destroyed her ability to function and always beclouded important issues. This prevented clarification and she was unable to extricate herself from a most vicious cycle. For years she actually regarded her manifestations of guilt as "responsibility" and couldn't understand why she couldn't change the situation. She had no idea that her guilt served as the most effective method she could develop to evade responsibility—for real self, decision and action.

I am not suggesting that healthy people ought not to have strong feelings about what's right and what's wrong. However, you can have them and act accordingly (and even better) without guilt. With a real feeling for self and for one's values, one must have real feelings for other people, too, so that guilt becomes both useless and destructive.

Guilt is also very cheap. Cheap because it is easily arrived at (anybody can feel guilty) and because, aside from pain, there is nothing derived from it. It is used as a substitute, block and dodge for real responsibility and, as such, is a detriment to successful relating. You simply cannot become a winner through the successful manufacture of guilt. In making a relationship successful, we are not interested in blame or affixing guilt or fault and following with punishment. This is not a mature approach to ourselves and it certainly isn't to other people. *Compassion*, both for ourselves and other people, and really caring, will mitigate guilt and self-hate (which only lower morale and have a weakening effect leading to further difficulty) and open the way for real responsibility, communication and growth.

Responsibility involves participating fully and realistically (with one's complete self) in the situation at hand, being cognizant that mistakes are made in life, having compassion for one's self and others, and being desirous of learning and growing from experience. "I am responsible" does not mean "I'll hate myself if I am wrong." It means that "I" will be responsible for myself and will participate as best I can.

Responsibility makes for mature decision-making and action. Or, in other words, *doing* and sometimes doing wrong. "I did it, I am responsible—nobody else. I don't hate myself for it or excoriate myself for it or feel a burden of guilt for it or dissipate energy in other sick pursuits. I want to know how come and what can be done." This makes investigation, growth and correction possible. Applied to relating, it is the antithesis of, "It was your fault," "No, it was yours," "Yes, it was mine," "No, you were right, it was mine." In relating it makes for statements like, "Well, what went wrong? How and what can we do about it?" Real responsibility for self in relating destroys self-recrimination and the projection of self-hate to others, thus contributing a great deal to possible success.

Why? what? how? when?

People, seemingly trying to find out about themselves and other people and their relating to other people, are constantly asking, why? Why this? Why that? Patients in psychotherapy ask this question again and again, convinced that the why of it will elucidate and resolve their problems. I think that the movies and television have contributed to this idea, too. They usually have a patient ask why this fear or that, or why this particular kind of behavior. Then the "psychiatrist" goes into a lengthy, supposedly curative, discourse.

The question of "why?" invariably leads to long intellectual explanations, discussions, and much psychologizing. While the discussion and discoursing may be about one person or the two people involved in the conversation, it sounds as though the two people are, in effect, discussing one or two people who are not actually there. The question "why?" leads to much logic and explanation about a subject connected to a person or people, but does not involve the people themselves. It is as if the discussion is going on at a great distance. This is largely because "why?" stimulates explanations springing from rationale and logic and very often is divorced from feelings. You will find that "what?" "when?" "how?" are much more valuable questions. Psychoanalysts are taught this very early in their training. They come to know that these questions elicit associations and thoughts which are linked to feelings and have the effect of extending old areas and opening up new ones. If John says, "I find Peter irritating," and you ask why, John is likely to answer, "I don't know" or "Oh, I just do," closing off the subject and any possibility of further insight. Or he may go on and say, "I think I get irritated when I'm confronted with immaturity in a domineering kind of person that I can do nothing about." While this may be true, it has no real value in improving the relationship between John and Peter.

But let us say you ask, "When did you find him irritating," and John says, "Last week when we were all out to dinner together." This immediately pinpoints an actual situation involving the two people and it triggers John's *feeling* about *what* happened rather than a logical theoretical explanation. If you then ask, "What happened," John may say, "Well, Peter was his usual self." "How so?" you may ask.

"Well, he picked up a menu and took over everything, insisting on ordering for everybody."

"*How* did you *feel?*" (*Feel* is much better than *think*.)

"I felt like really telling him off. I felt like taking the damned menu and hitting him with it. But, of course, I didn't. I sat there and did nothing. God, I've done that often enough in the past."

"*What?*"

"Sitting and taking it when I could have done something about it or at least spoken up."

"*When?*"

"Well, with my father for one, who always took over and never let people fend for themselves. I never told

119

him off, either. To this day, he has no more idea how irritating he could be than Peter has."

"*How* come he has no idea?"

"I guess nobody has ever told him, least of all me. I really ought to tell people *how* I feel—clear the air—so I don't go around feeling rotten about it."

Thus John has come to several valuable insights about his relating to people, among them:

1) That he tends to repeat a pattern with domineering people that was first established with his father.

2) That he has difficulty telling these people that he is irritated.

3) That if you don't tell them they don't know, and there is no opportunity to improve communications and relations.

These insights, ultimately worked with, again and again, will open new areas and link up to other insights. This will make for personal growth, as well as much more successful relating. Experience has taught me that "why" simply does not produce this kind of feeling and growing. Intellectualizing and psychologizing in an effort to find explanations do not lead to a growing experience or to constructive possibilities. Seeking for time, feelings and feeling-laden experiences and memories *does* make for the possibility of growth.

Too few of us are concerned with these *feeling* questions—the *what, how* and *when* of it. We are overly concerned with the logic and thinking out the *why* of it. The fact is that when the *whats, whens* and *hows* are worked out, real *knowing* on a deep level, making change possible, takes place. In this kind of knowing, the intellectual knowing, the why becomes apparent, too. It is there as a natural by-product without being asked for.

So, don't please get hooked on *why* this or that and on long, theoretical logical explanations about you and your behavior, let alone about you and your ways of relating. If you do, it will have the same effect as talking about a Broadway play. If you really want to find out and improve and be a winner with Max, then you must get involved with feelings. Believe me, this is best done by asking yourself *what* you felt, *how* you felt, *when* did you feel it? In what way did you feel it? What actually happened between you and Max? Did it remind you of anything? What? How? When? Anything else? What? How? When?

I would die for this

My good friend and great teacher, Dr. Nathan Freeman, has always had a way of inventing provocative questions that open up and illuminate important and interesting areas of human behavior. One of his questions was, "People always say they are willing to die for this or that cause or that they would gladly die for a son or daughter if it became necessary. How come I don't hear more of them say that they are willing to LIVE for something?"

I'm sure that many people mean what they say quite literally. There are numerous examples of people who have sacrificed their lives for other people, causes and principles. Of course, other people use this as a form of superlative emphasis to express their feelings about issues and persons about which and for whom their interest and concern couldn't be stronger. But I feel that Dr. Freeman knew that the statement had meaning and reflected feelings that are not at once obvious, and I quite agree with him.

My own belief is that people are confused about loyalty and dedication. Interestingly, we often see ourselves making grand, melodramatic and sacrificial gestures. The gestures are sometimes made in the service of martyrdom and consist of suffering and even death. This points to a blatant confusion because there is hardly a cause, principle or person that would not derive much more benefit from a living benefactor rather than a dead one. Frankly, I suspect that a "willingness to die for someone" is most often linked to Christlike self-glorification and has little to do with altruistic desires.

To care—to really care—to care enough to invest feelings and emotions and to give service, too, and to be thoroughly involved in and with, one must be very much alive. It takes aliveness, total aliveness, to help somebody.

I have known people in great pain, suffering from lingering, debilitating diseases who, for themselves, really wanted an end to come. But these few people fought to keep alive, at great self-sacrifice, because they felt they had a job to do for the benefit of others. These people were not seeking immortality or self-glorification. Living was a terrible burden to them but, in effect, they were saying, "I care so much for you—that I'd gladly live for you." Yes, to really care is to be life-oriented and to be life-oriented is to really care. Caring and relating and being involved with Max here and Max there is the stuff of life—and the more real relating that takes place, the less likely it is that we will see death as a commodity of value.

Death, hurting others and peace

"I'll be dead and then you'll be sorry." Have you heard this before? Many people feel suicidal at some point in their lives, others have suicidal thoughts at times, but, fortunately, a relatively small percentage actually attempt suicide. Many of these thoughts and feelings come from a buried desire for freedom from problems, woes and burdens. Very often, suprisingly, a vacation will help to allay these thoughts.

However, there are people who seriously consider and even attempt suicide "to be at peace." Well, let's blast this muddle. Doing so can be life-saving. Suicide equals death, but death and peace have nothing whatsoever to do with each other. With due respect to the minister who says, "May she rest in peace," there is neither peace nor rest in death. In death, there is an end to things and ways and feelings that are born of life. Peace and rest are very much states of living and feeling—and are linked to aliveness.

As a matter of fact, they are luxuries of life, not easily arrived at and attained only with considerable work. Yes, just as you must be alive to feel excitement, joy, warmth, cold, loving, you must be alive to feel at rest and at peace. Death brings an end to feelings of contentment, wonder, warmth, peace and rest. The wonderful feeling of peace can never be attained through suicide.

"I'll die and then you'll be sorry" is not an infrequent motivation for suicide. Suicide, committed with this motivation, is an extremely vindictive act (vindictive to self and to Max). It is an attempt to make other people feel guilty and regretful. It often has its earliest roots in childhood fantasies of being sick and having everybody around one's bed, wringing their hands in despair and regret for all the wrongs committed against the now desperately sick patient. There is also a kind of self-glorification in this process, which one sees in similar forms in related areas. It is also an attempt to manipulate Max (to get him to do something); but Max may get pretty sick of it all and walk out. I am reminded of the elderly mother who says, "Go out and have a wonderful time. Whatever you do, don't worry about me. What if I do fall down the stairs while you are gone? I'll just lie there until you come back. But please, don't think about me—not even for a second—just make sure you have a good time."

"I'll be dead, then you will be sorry" is closely linked to "rest in peace" in the unreality they both share. The desired effect of "I'll be dead" is to get back at Max—to make him miserable, to get even, and to deprive him of your company. In short, to be as vindictive as possible. *But* vindictiveness, however destructive, is also a human feeling requiring aliveness. The dead are dead and feel nothing and cannot feel, let alone derive any satisfaction (however illusory) from a vindictive act.

The would-be suicide (a dead person, if successful) has the magical delusion that in some mysterious way she will be present after death to enjoy Max's pain at her recent demise. But no matter how much Max may mourn, she will not be there to "enjoy" it! You have to be alive to be there!

Big emotional displays are evidence of deep feelings

There are people who emote readily and who feel deeply and strongly, but there are at least as many (and, I suspect, more) who do not flaunt emotions, who cannot make big scenes, and who also feel very strongly and deeply.

To feel does not necessarily mean to overtly express feelings. Demonstrations of feelings, loud and strong—tears, rage, blood and thunder—do not mean that one feels. Many people cover up an inability to feel with an overlay of great emotional display, just as many women cover up an inability to respond sexually with particularly seductive dress, carriage, walk and talk. By the same token, people who respond readily with great emotional display, are no more sensitive than people who are more self-contained about their feelings.

Great emotional acts are also very often diversionary maneuvers designed to cover up other feelings entirely. At times, the individual who is reacting is not really aware of what she is feeling. The cover-up is used, not only to fool Max, but herself as well, so that she can hide unwanted feelings from herself.

In order to better understand most people it is more important to listen to the music than the words. But in attempting to understand "big emoters," it is often quite the reverse—one must listen to the words. The truly impressive emoters (hysterical outbursts, etc.) usually say little with their outbursts, but they will let a few words slip here and there which may clue you to what they really mean. You must listen closely and learn to put the clues together.

Let me tell you about a kind of corollary phenomenon here, namely the business of overreacting or reacting with inappropriate intensity. If Max, whoever he is, reacts very intensely to a situation that doesn't call for this kind of big emotion, you can bet he is not reacting to this situation (or to you) at all. He is reacting to another situation or person, perhaps from the distant past, and he may not be aware of it at all. So, if you can keep from getting hooked into a logical or rational argument (concerning the present situation which he is reacting to on the surface), by all means do so, because logic will avail you nothing. You will simply be talking about something which is not the cause of the emoting at all. It may just be the trigger or the reminder.

Let me end my discussion of this muddle with this last observation. Now and then, you will run into people who will "tell you all about yourself." These are the unpaid and untrained *psychoanalyzers* (I reserve the terms analyst or psychoanalyst for professionals who will not analyze you without payment—except in a clinic, and who will never analyze you in public). These people do a great deal of psychologizing and intellectualizing and much of it is an attempt to impress you, themselves or any audience present. They also use this "analyzing" as a means of expressing hostility, vindictiveness—"shaking you up"—under the guise of being nice to you; they are "honestly" telling you about yourself and your problems—for your own good, of course. The best way to handle this kind of person is to tell him that you will pay a psychoanalyst for an analytic consultation, if you want one, just as you would pay for a surgical consultation if you wanted one; or just walk out. You stand to gain nothing from this kind of "analysis."

If, however, you should have any desire to learn about the analyzer, then stay and listen. In telling you about you, he will be projecting many bits and fragments about himself. If you listen closely and pick up the various subtleties and have a knack for putting these things together, you will learn much about your would-be analyst.

One last hint. If he becomes particularly vituperative or strong in emotional displays listen very closely because he will then be particularly revealing—about himself.

Pride—sick or healthy?

The concept of pride (and the investment of pride in things, causes, areas, etc.) and its ramifications has been part of man's history since the dawn of civilization. The Greeks knew that "pride goeth before a fall" and they demonstrated it admirably in the classical Greek dramas. Historians and sociologists have for years concerned themselves with studies of national pride. Of course, psychoanalysts have been fascinated with pride and its role in human behavior (some of it pretty sick) and have written many papers about it.

I feel that this muddle—between sick pride and healthy pride—is one of the most prevalent and destructive of all. I hear references to pride again and again by parents, teachers, politicians. From what they say I know that many of them don't realize the difference between sick and healthy pride and, more often than not, are advising, pushing and selling sick pride. So let's dig into this at least a little bit.

Sick pride is always linked to glory. People invest pride in this or that activity for the purpose of self-glorification. This need for self-glorification is born of great feelings of inadequacy, and since the pride covers up those feelings, but in no way changes them, this drive becomes an insatiable taskmaster. (The glory can be derived from martyrdom or power or both. If it is both, the individual feels literally torn apart.)

For example, let us say that a man compensates for a feeling of inadequacy by dreams of being extraordinarily wealthy. His image of himself is that of a multimillionaire admired by all as a self-made giant. In this case, we would say that Mr. Smith has pride invested in making money. Now, no matter how much money Smith makes, it will not mitigate his feelings of inadequacy (which come from sources entirely removed from fiscal impoverishment), which will go on plaguing him (often without his knowledge or awareness). He will be driven to greater and greater excesses in the exploitation of himself and others to attain an unreachable goal—even into a heart attack and death, because no amount of money will suffice. The glory he attains will be fleeting and paltry compared with that which he continues to need (e.g., Hitler: had he conquered the world, the moon would have been next and even the universe could not have been enough).

Now, should this man's pride be hurt, should he suffer a business reversal, he is no longer protected from his feelings of inadequacy or from his enormous self-hate (generated from those feelings and designed to push him to greater glory to escape them), which, unleashed, generates much anxiety, depression and projected rage at those whom he sees as the attackers of his pride. This, of course, is a vast oversimplification, because what happens depends on what its part is in an intricate network of breached defenses and responses—some very subtle and some quite blatant. However, we are only using this as an example. Thus sick pride always involves a shield protecting hidden fragility, as part of an insatiable and compulsive (Smith must do it—he has no choice) drive for glory and self-aggrandizement, be it through power or martyrdom. Hurt pride is an affront to the image or role one sets for himself to offset the image of himself which he hates and which represents his feelings of inadequacy and worthlessness. So each time sick pride is hurt—that is, pride that bolsters his image—he becomes aware of his hated self. Thus, hurt sick pride results in anxiety and anger: anger in the form of self-hate and hate for whoever he thinks is hurting his pride. I believe, as do many of my colleagues, that hurt sick pride accounts for most suicides, as well as nearly all murders, excluding some of those with a dollar motive. Explanations involving sick pride are masterfully discussed by Karen Horney in her various works.

In healthy pride, we do things for the fun of it, for the good feelings that come of it, for the joys in feelings of self-accomplishment. Jones makes money to enjoy the security it brings his family and to enjoy the things it brings him. He feels good about making it, but that feeling good is a personal issue in which he does not seek out the admiration of others or mastery over them, let alone their exploitation. Unlike Smith, he is the master of money and not vice versa. He has a choice and values his self and life more than the attainment of a goal. Therefore, he does not kill himself in the pursuit of power through money. Business reversals do not put him in touch with a hated, inadequate image any more than business success protected or shielded him from this image. Business failure does not result in feelings of doom, great rage, anxiety, suicide or murder. This is not to say that he is happy about them or that he takes them with equanimity. This would be as inappropriate as Smith's reaction. He is unhappy about a situation that is obviously detrimental to his well-being, but he is not shattered—a dream of glory has not been smashed—he did not fall from fantastic (and I do mean fantasy here) heights, because his feet never left the ground in the first place.

I want to close discussion on this muddle by saying that here again there are no blacks and whites. We all of us have some neurotic pride—that is, areas where it operates. In some of us, it is stronger than in others. All of us have feelings of healthy, spontaneous (noncompulsive) self-accomplishment. There is a little of Jones and Smith in all of us. The ratio is very important as is an individual's general background, behavior and integrated assets. Knowing the difference, however, is very important. When you know that you are reacting to hurt pride it gives you the opportunity to look and see where this hurt is coming from and affords the opportunity to explore further and to grow, so that sick pride can more and more be replaced by healthy pride.

If you feel that you are reacting very strongly and inappropriately to criticism or something someone says, then chances are 99 out of 100 a sick pride has been hurt. If Max responds this way, then the same is true of him. The questions here—What was hurt? How did this knock me or Max down? How come? What was I protecting? This can lead to much illumination and even to a healthy, practical, self-enhancing response to what might turn out to be constructive criticism.

Psychoanalysis and health equals happiness

"Health and successful psychoanalysis should result in constant happiness." This is simply not true. Again and again, I see people who regard emotional health as pure and perfect happiness, and who feel that psychoanalysis has that goal in mind. Of course, nobody is perfectly healthy and nobody is perfectly analyzed. But, no matter how healthy or well analyzed, constant happiness would be completely inappropriate and surely a sign of some great inner paralysis. As a matter of fact, health and analysis do make for a greater ability for happiness, but they also make for a range of healthy and appropriate emotional responses. People are confused in that they somehow think that only happy responses are healthy ones. Of course, this is not true. Health and analytic treatment for the attainment of greater health extend the whole range of emotions and make for the appropriate use of all emotions. Of course, this includes a response of sorrow to tragic situations. However, in health, these responses will never be overwhelming, chronic or shattering. We have them and then go on living and using our whole emotional range in response to all else life has to offer.

I would just like to say here that one of the goals of psychoanalysis certainly includes a greater capacity for happiness through a better handling of problems. But psychoanalysis does not remove the generation of problems. As long as we live, we will have them; this is an inherent part of the human condition. Hopefully, we can handle problems as they come up, healthfully and constructively, so that we can grow through their resolution.

Self-pity and self-chastisement

These are simply not the same and yet they are confused nearly all of the time. Again and again, I hear people say, "I'm so full of self-pity, I can't stand myself" or I hear "analyzers" (or would-be analysts) tell people, "You are so swamped with self-pity you are drowning in it—stop pitying yourself and do something about yourself that's worthwhile." Well, in 99 percent of these cases, they are not talking about self-pity at all. They are talking about self-chastisement, self-berating, self-derision. It often goes something like this, "I just can't stand myself. I look at myself in the mirror and I'm ugly—I'm so stupid—I feel so blue all of the time—how can anybody as inept as me get on in this world?" At times, there may be a nuance of pity here and there, but I would call this a pseudo self-pity—it is really all self-chastisement. Self-pity would go like this, "I feel depressed, I find it difficult to do even the simplest things right now, so I'm going to take it particularly easy with myself. I'm going to rest and work at finding out what gives, so I can get to feel better." What is the difference between these two approaches? Well, they come of entirely different mamas and have entirely different purposes.

Self-chastisement is born of self-hate, is a destructive force which never takes mitigating circumstances into account, is harsh and full of harassment, cares more for the greater glory and idealization of the individual than for his real welfare.

Self-pity—real self-pity (not neurotic, compulsive self-pity which is really a perverted form of self-hate or the complicated variety seen in hypochondriacs)—is born of compassion for self, is constructive, is chiefly concerned with the individual's survival and welfare, and is very much aware of the total picture, including mitigating circumstances like pain, sickness or limitations (temporary as well as otherwise).

When a patient says to me, "I'm so full of self-pity, I can't stomach myself," I usually say, "Well, you have a strange way of showing it. If you had a friend who was suffering, I doubt that you'd say that you can't stand him. You would really pity him and have compassion for him and patience with him. How about coming down from your lofty glorious perch long enough to have some compassion and patience for yourself?" I may then go on to give the following example: John fractures his leg. It is a simple uncomplicated fracture. But John despises himself for having the accident in the first place, feeling that people like himself should never have accidents. He particularly hates his leg which is a reminder of his infirmity and his mortality. So he says, "Look at me, look at me sitting here like a cripple, all full of self-pity. I can't stand the sight of myself—to break a leg, what a stupid thing to do—damned leg—look at it." With this statement, John gets increasingly angry and then becomes so enraged that he pounds his leg with his fist. This compounds the fracture, turning a simple condition into a serious one, which will take much longer to heal. When John realizes what he has done, he is filled with even greater self-loathing, thus completing a very destructive vicious cycle. Jim, on the other hand, also has a simple leg fracture with no complications. But Jim's attitude is different. He has not demanded everlasting immortal glory for himself. He knows that he is human and that humans have limitations and accidents. He has compassion for human foibles, including his own, and is aware that things happen over which he has no control, since it is realistically impossible to totally control one's environment. So Jim says in effect, "This is my leg—it is part of me and I like me—and that includes an injured me. My poor leg is broken. It really is a pity, I'm going to take particularly good care of it until it is completely healed." He then has it treated and is mindful of his temporary infirmity and limitations; his leg therefore heals quickly and uneventfully without complication of any sort.

Of course, the same is true of emotional upsets and problems. Self-chastisement, as well as chastisement from others, blocks healing and healthy growth. Self-pity (not the taunting variety which is pseudo self-pity) born of real compassion for self and cognizant of the limitations in being human leads to healing and growth.

Accomplishment

To arrive at a desired goal or to achieve something is an accomplishment, *but* accomplishment is relative to the individual and to his particular condition at a given time. This sounds simple enough and so obvious as to be unworthy of discussion. But, believe me, when I say that the vast majority of people do not see it this way at all. Unfortunately, most people have distorted concepts of what is and isn't an accomplishment. This is a pity because they destroy the possibility of deriving enjoyment and self-esteem from many, many daily accomplishments.

Many people are unaware that daily functioning is full of accomplishments in the fulfillment of thousands of goals—dressing, washing, preparing food, telephoning, shopping, etc., etc. All this is taken for granted without seeming awareness that *everybody in fact cannot* do it. People rob themselves of the joy of a sense of accomplishment (a healthy pride) largely because they secretly think of accomplishment almost exclusively in terms of great public prestige and recognition. They have an absolute base line in mind, that is, a picture of what fulfills the requirements necessary for any act to be an "accomplishment" and there is almost no feeling of relative gradation about it.

Feelings of accomplishment are further weakened and destroyed by a general feeling of low self-esteem. This often goes something like this: "If I accomplished it, how important can it be? Must be nothing at all." This is another way of saying, "Anything is important until I do it. When I've done it, it turns to nothing." Some of the manifestations are more subtle. They go like this: "I don't know—I think I'm interested and really want it. Soon as I get it, I couldn't care less." Actually, these statements indicate very poor self-esteem and also a defense against this feeling of inadequacy, namely, inordinate feelings of grandiosity. In effect, the individual is saying, "Whatever I do is nothing because it doesn't compare to what I ought to do if fitted in with my exalted superman picture of myself. Besides, how can it be worth anything if lowly me did it?" Thus, he leaves himself no possibility of deriving satisfaction from a sense of accomplishment. He is driven to greater and greater glories in an effort to feel a sense of accomplishment, when he is in fact accomplishing much every day.

Accomplishments are relative to particular people, to particular situations and to particular times. This seems obvious, but people instantly forget it. We are, in fact, so apt to forget it that I feel it is important to stress it again here.

When we are sick, we can't do as much as when we are well. Doing a little when we are sick is often more than the equivalent of doing more when we are well. For a man who has had a paralyzing stroke to be able to begin to walk is a considerable accomplishment and he must walk before he can run. If he sees walking as no accomplishment at all—"something any child can do"—his lack of sense of accomplishment will destroy his motivation, feed his hopelessness and may well arrest his progress. I remember a man who had a very severe phobia which prevented him from moving out of a particular ten-block area for over ten years. After working very hard in treatment for several years, he was able to rid himself of this phobia enough so that he could go anywhere at any time, without anxiety. His mother, a very destructive woman, responded to his enormous accomplishment (which freed him to go on to make progress in other areas) with the statement, "Now you can do what any ten-year-old can do." Fortunately the man did not need outside corroboration to "feel" a sense of accomplishment. He "knew" what he had done—and "knowing" in terms of *self,* motivated him to do still more.

Owning what you've got—bragging—compulsive modesty

When somebody owns what he's got—a particular asset, ability, or accomplishment—he more than knows about it. It is his—in his guts—and he feels it as part and parcel of himself (see introduction to Section I). Then he doesn't need to brag about having it. If he does brag, then it is obvious that he does not own it— at least not fully—because his bragging is an attempt at self-reassurance that he does in fact own it. The more he brags the more shaky he is about the very thing he is bragging about. It is as if he must have a response (usually of awe) from somebody other than himself in order to be reassured. Since no kind of reassurance will give him a sense of ownership, which is only born of increased self-esteem, he usually goes on bragging and seeking outside reassurance in order to be convinced. Now compulsive modesty is also evidence of a lack of ownership because here, too, the non-owning owner compulsively seeks reassurance of ownership. The very act of repeated expressions of modesty is designed to elicit direct words of emphasis and reassurance. A real owner does not go about "blowing his own horn" nor does he "put himself down" vis-à-vis Max. He is what he is, knows who he is, knows what he's got and presents himself accordingly, without any need for stratagems designed to get Max to tell him about what a great guy he is. The fact is that he does not need medals and does not seek them. He doesn't seek them through attempts at charming and overpowering people, and he doesn't seek them through attempts at modesty, sometimes carried to the extreme point of misery and martyrdom. So there is neither the bravado of "I'll show you what a terrific guy I am" nor the self-effacing "Well, I've known some pretty hard times and I guess I'm just not very good at anything." Ownership (when you've really got what you've got) negates any need for duplicitous machinations and manipulations. Owners don't attempt to exploit Max—to use him—as one or another kind of "yes man," and the relationship between owners is a mature one. Energy isn't expended on compulsive demands and expressions of reassurance. I have known people who unwittingly were in the presence of chronic non-owners and came away feeling "weakened," "emptied," "sucked dry," "enervated," without knowing why. The truth is that they had in fact been "exploited and emptied" by being manipulated by the non-owner (who also did this unconsciously) into giving reassurance again and again, either by expressions of awe or great ap-

137

preciation or direct expressions of reassurance—"Oh, come on, you must know that you are more capable than that." On a continued basis, both bragging and compulsive modesty are very taxing to a relationship with Max and ultimately very destructive. However, non-ownership can exist in various degrees with more or less blatant and very subtle manifestations. Relating to owners —real owners—is so much more easy, direct, noncontrived and refreshingly spontaneous.

Arrogance and humility

We all have had experience with arrogance in one form or another, in ourselves as well as in other people. There are some people in whom arrogance is almost a way of life. Sometimes we have very strong responses to them—"I hate him," "He's so God-damned obnoxious," "A very powerful and overwhelming personality," etc. In any case, there is much confusion and misunderstanding about arrogance and therefore great difficulty in relating to arrogant people or to people when they are arrogant.

I've heard arrogance confused with wisdom, strength, great expertise, absolute ownership, great self-esteem, talent, extraordinary ability, stupidity, meanness, hate, inhumanity, innate brutality, inordinate sadistic tendencies, rage, hostility, etc. While there may be elements of any of these in an arrogant individual, we may also find one or more of these characteristics in people who couldn't be less arrogant.

What is arrogance about? Why does an individual

arrogate or ascribe to himself or take unto himself special privileges or powers or demands? What does arrogance come from? The answer is *fear*. Analysts again and again find that arrogant people are people who are extremely fearful, who feel extremely weak and fragile and who cover up their fear with arrogance. If arrogance is very pronounced—that is, if we are dealing with an individual who is almost always arrogant—then we are dealing with a very fragile person indeed. When the "arrogant" person is even more arrogant than usual, you can bet that he is feeling particularly threatened and if not actually weakened, then potentially weakened. One can argue that arrogance is perhaps a cultural phenomenon. Witness Nazi Germany where whole populations of people arrogated all kinds of special Aryan characteristics to themselves, where a swaggering walk was almost a national characteristic. My answer is that here too, arrogance covered up enormous feelings of lack of identity, lack of values, lack of feelings of self (in this case, almost complete lack of identity with being human), great weakness and feelings of being threatened to the point of paranoia on a mass or national scale. If the weakness felt is great enough, then the special characteristics (and demands based on these special characteristics) ascribed to self become greater and greater. Thus in Germany, the Nazis covered up feelings of worthlessness, emptiness, inner collapse, and self-degradation with delusions of grandeur and superiority (a master race). On an individual basis, arrogance also sometimes goes from the neurotic to the psychotic loss of reality, in which individuals see themselves as all powerful, having special powers, being one or another "great man" or being God himself. Psychoanalysts know about the fragility of very arrogant people and are therefore extremely careful in treating them. Patients in whom arrogance is a way of life can be extremely expert at bait-ing and goading. There may be a great temptation on the part of the therapist to take the bait and to "put them down once and for all," but they don't do this because they know that these fragile people can be terribly hurt very easily, making treatment much longer and more difficult, if not impossible. You may have experienced a similar phenomenon as a youngster in dealing with a bully. A confrontation with a bully usually results in an immediate capitulation and collapse since you unwittingly put him in touch with feelings of great weakness and raw fear. I remember this happening and then feeling so sorry for the bully that I felt compelled to reassure him that he was a worthwhile guy after all. I can understand this now in terms of the feelings of weakness, self-hate and awful fear (of being found out) that lurks just below the surface arrogance.

Now, what about humility? Humility is only too often confused with weakness, fear, stupidity, lacks of all kinds in all departments—compulsive modesty, servility, apple-polishing, compulsive humbling, humiliation, self-effacement and compliance. Of course this is not the case at all. Compulsive modesty, self-effacement and compliance are born of a need to be liked and to seek glory through martyrdom. This is the result of feeling inadequate and weak and having a poor sense of ownership in regard to one's assets. At rock bottom the basis for this behavior is much the same as for arrogance. However, humility is born of different stuff entirely. Humility is born of strength. People with real humility have no need to browbeat others into subservience in order to convince themselves of their prowess. They have no need for reassurance as regards ability, lovability or assets. They know who they are, what they stand for, have definite values, a strong sense of identity, excellent ownership and great resiliency. They are self-accepting and accepting of others. Then real humility never operates in the service of martyrdom. It operates as a sureness of self with "nothing to prove." People with real humility are not sensitive to criticism. They are open to suggestion and learning without being suggestible. They are capable of growth and the best possible relationships with Max. In people who have real humility there is little evidence of sick pride. With humility, we find concomitant health and strength and self-acceptance, all the antithesis of sick pride. Sick pride goes hand in hand with vulnerability, chronic hurt feelings and fear of people. The less sick pride one has the better his relating to himself and the rest of the world will be.

Courage and cowardice

There is at least as much confusion about something called "courage" as there is about strength and weakness, which is considerable. In analyzing people and seeing them very closely over extended periods of time, many of the confusions and subsequent demands on others and one's self become apparent. Courage is confused with strength. It is confused with masculinity, brutality, suffering and martyrdom, foolhardiness, a disregard for self and a love of danger, patriotism, athletic prowess, racism, love of war, a capacity to kill, etc., etc. I feel that what we call "courage" is highly individual and relative to our own standards, fears and idealizations. I think the term is a highly judgmental one, for the most part born of a need for self, group or national glorification. I feel that in a society where man accepts himself and

141

accepts his fellows there is relatively little stress placed on "courage" as a virtue. I believe that caring and responsibility are more indicative of health than courage. When one cares enough about one's self and about one's fellows (Max), then he will demonstrate that "caring" in acts that may be called "courageous."

A corollary of the courage morass is the *cowardice* one. Frankly, I feel that this, too, is a highly judgmental term often used and born of great hypocrisy. I feel that this term is often applied to people who are either honest and open enough to admit to having particular fears or to people who have inordinate fears. I see no constructive rationale in calling particularly fearful people "cowards" or other derogatory terms. Very fearful people are sick people and ought to be treated with compassion and consideration. I might say here that I have found a good many heroes who were very sick people, too, in some ways not too far removed from sick people who became murderers.

In a world where war still prevails, where there are any number of breakdowns in communications, where people still kill people in large numbers for any number of reasons, it perhaps behooves us to reevaluate some of our ideas concerning courage and cowardice.

In this connection, I would like to square away another confusion. Many people see *surrender* as a passive and "cowardly" act. Well, let me say that in surrender, as with passive resistance, great energy and strength are often necessary. It is sometimes necessary, appropriate, and wise to surrender now in order to win later. Fighters will lose a round or take the count, in order to rest and get up at the count of nine to go on and win. I would like to apply this to emotional upsets. If you are in a particularly poor mood, feeling very anxious or quite depressed, it is often wise not to fight it, not to carry on—

stiff upper lip, go on working, etc. On the contrary, as difficult as it is, surrender to the sickness—taking off from work, treating oneself gently, restfully, with a vacation and a convalescence, much as you would do with a physical illness—may be very valuable. To surrender to great fatigue and to take off and to rest despite a lifetime habit of "going on at any cost" can save your life. Doing this, however, may be impossible if one is confused about courage, heroism and other sweeping judgmental concepts.

Another confusion that ought to be handled in this connection is the one pertaining to *self-preservation*. Let me say, as I indicated earlier, that interest in self to the exclusion of all others and all else points to serious emotional difficulties. Since this destroys success in relating to Max, it can hardly be deemed as self-preservation. But there is nothing sick about a desire for self-preservation existing with a concomitant concern for others. Self-preservation is often seen as opportunism, selfishness, cowardice, etc. It is no such thing. It springs from a healthy regard for self and the basic need, desire and identification with the human race and its continued existence.

Temptation and succumbing to temptation

Many people, without real awareness, demand the impossible and inhuman of themselves. They, in fact, feel that they should not be tempted (sexually, moneywise, etc.) at all, and attempt to deny that they are tempted or look upon themselves with great disdain if their temptations are revealed to themselves. This need to be purer than pure, to not be tempted, is largely due to a need to glorify oneself to saintlike proportions. It also springs from the confusion that temptation and succumbing to temptation are one and the same thing. Well, there are no wings on our backs, we are not angels, we are human and I suspect the same was true of the saints. Perhaps they coped with temptations with greater control than most of us can, but they surely had temptations. Otherwise how were they saintly? In any case, we all have temptations, but temptations and action or succumbing is not the same thing. We may be tempted, but whether we go ahead or not will be another matter. Now the more sense of values, identity, self we have, the more capable we will be in making a decision—a constructive decision in regard to temptations. *But* what will give us particular freedom of choice and self-control in our decision will be a conscious awareness of being tempted in the first place. The more we hide from the temptation, the more we attempt to deny having it, the more judgmental we are about having it—the less choice we will have regarding it. It will control us rather than us it. The more we can admit our humanity, our human limitations and our temptations, the better able we will be to openly and freely cope with them. The less judgmental we are and the more accepting we are of ourselves and all of our feelings and temptations, whatever they are, the better able we will be to make constructive decisions in our own behalf and for the good solid success of all our relationships.

Choice and compulsion

Many people operate in their daily lives as automatons, almost completely unaware that their nearly every action is dictated by compulsion, with little or no freedom of choice and with virtually no spontaneity. Many people don't know the difference between compulsion and choice.

Compulsion refers to behavior that is stilted, rigid, patterned, with little or no possibility of flexibility or variation. Regardless of whether the behavior is a small repeated ritualistic act (washing one's hands every five minutes) or a larger, broader way of behavior (in relating to people), compulsive behavior is always a defense against anxiety and becomes accentuated in times of anxiety. In behaving compulsively the individual responds to a contract (set of learned rules) he has with himself and which he must not break. He may be aware of being compulsive or having a compulsion without any awareness of the contract or his anxiety or he may also be unaware of being compulsive. In any case, his blind allegiance to the contract permits no deviation, and any infraction at all is immediately punishable by an upsurge of anxiety (sleeplessness, loss of appetite, overeating, palpitations, stomach upsets, feelings of tension and uneasiness), self-hate, self-contempt, derision and chastisement and depression.

Choice is just that. One can and does choose what, how and where without being cramped by the coercion of an inner tyranny. There is no contract. One can weigh and measure an issue and can determine with his whole being what his choice of behavior will be. There is

145

flexibility, variation and growth, as well as the possibility of fluctuation, changing one's mind and making mistakes without repercussions. Regardless of the choice and its outcome, there is freedom of movement, and action is not followed by anxiety or depression because there is no contract and no taskmaster. Choice is not born of an old learned "acceptable" pattern. It is born spontaneously of the contact of the complete individual and the particular situation that he finds himself in. Please do not confuse spontaneous behavior with impulsive behavior. They couldn't be more opposite. Spontaneous behavior taps the whole of an individual in his free response to a particular issue or situation. He is free to take more or less time in making his spontaneous decision. In any case, he's *free* and makes his decision unfettered by anxiety-producing rigidified (old learned) contracts. Impulsive behavior is born of the moment, *but* it is a response to being a slave to compulsion. It is either a poor attempt to sneak some pseudo-free or pseudo-spontaneous behavior quickly past the guard of the compulsion contract, or in other cases, it is a rebellion against compulsion. Many people are so overwhelmed and tyrannized by their compulsions that they must act out (do things) immediately, impulsively, without thought or consideration in order to overcome complete and utter paralysis.

I would like to point out here that in nearly all issues and situations, there is at least one or more choices. People who cannot discern the choices, who feel that there is only one possible route (often the most destructive one), who feel trapped and often anxiety-ridden because of their feeling of entrapment, who feel that they cannot even see the possibility of postponement of action, let alone postponement of decision, are invariably people who are trapped in the compulsive tyranny of one or another (or a generalized) contract with themselves. This

146

is the antithesis of spontaneity. When an individual is spontaneous, he can see more than one course of action; he can postpone action until he sees more and until issues become clarified. Being confronted with several choices and/or postponements does not make him anxious, does not make him feel that a sword is hanging over his head or that a very urgent noncompromising contract will be broken.

If you are not sure whether or not a particular course of action is compulsive, you've only to ask yourself, "Will not doing it or taking an alternate course make me feel a lot of anxiety?" If the answer is *no,* then the decision leading to the action and the action itself at least has the possibility of having been born of healthy spontaneous choice.

Self-acceptance

Many people have confused ideas about what this all-important term means. There's no point in going into all the confusing ramifications. Let us better spend our time constructively by clarifying its meaning. That we do so is all-important because lack of self-acceptance greatly impinges on our ability to either accept or relate (successfully) to Max. Self-acceptance is absolutely crucial to growth, change and an improved ability to relate.

Some people in analytic treatment often say, "OK, I admit that I'm this way or that" under the impression that in that statement they are expressing self-acceptance. Well, admitting "something" about one's self can be an initial step in self-acceptance, but it is not enough and very often this "admission" smacks of the very antithesis of acceptance. "Admission" can even indicate guilt, reluctance to accept and potential self-chastisement. Acceptance of one's self is nonjudgmental and nonselective. This means that one accepts all that goes on in him and not just those aspects that are socially "passable." He does not exclude those aspects which may not be socially approved or those aspects that he would rather not have. He does not pass judgment and say this is good or this is bad. This also includes those things about himself that are neurotic and even destructive. Dr. Nathan Freeman says, "You have to love your neurosis in order to get over it." Strange as this sounds, he is perfectly right. It is the story of the broken leg again. Aspects of ourselves that are neurotic are nevertheless parts of ourselves. Hating those parts of ourselves only creates self-hate and beclouds already beclouded issues. Self-judgment, moralizing and chastising do not make these aspects of ourselves go away any more than an attempt to evade or to bury them does. "Loving" ourselves in all our ramifications, including that which is sick in ourselves, affords us the opportunity to look, listen, feel and to use our energy to change, if we so desire. In effect, we are then saying, "Yes, I get into this kind of destructive relationship again and again. There is something sick here. But it is me and I don't hate me. So what gives and what can I do?" Self-acceptance is sometimes confused with resignation. Again —they couldn't be more different. Resignation or resigning involves giving up the possibility of growth or change. This is a compulsive process, the result of anxiety and an attempt to allay anxiety by no longer caring—by permanently giving up—and in effect by removing oneself as much as possible from relating experiences. In resigning, the individual has already judged himself and judged himself to be "so bad" that he's resigned from potential struggle and growth. In self-acceptance, the individual says quite the reverse. He says, "I am I, and whatever I am, I accept me as me. Now how can I take what I am and use what I am in the service of better health, better relating and greater happiness?" Self-acceptance is born of hope, spontaneity and the belief in the possibility of change.

Getting better or healthier and getting cured

This is a confusion that pertains to a black or white outlook again. However, this is a black and white outlook that involves a particularly important issue. People think in terms of complete and absolute resolution of their problems. I speak here of problems relative to themselves and those relative to other people. They think of an all or nothing situation in which there is sickness and either the possibility of utter hopelessness or complete cure. Since it is almost always impossible to envision a complete cure, they are often reluctant to undertake any constructive program at all. Well, let's face it— there are very few absolute or complete cures, just as there is no absolute sick or healthy state (only a combination of both). This applies to most areas of medicine and is particularly true of personality problems, emotional problems and problems in relating to Max. We are not machines and will never achieve perfection. *But* we can get better or healthier. We can change. We can resolve problems. We can achieve relative maturity and success and happiness in better relating to ourselves and to others. Residuals of old problems and bad habits may exist for years, but growth toward greater health can take place at the same time. Let me say here and now that "getting better" doesn't happen suddenly. Insight and getting better at relating to self and to others take time. Like education, which happens all through one's schooling and not just at the moment of being handed a diploma, getting better does not occur suddenly and climactically. It is a gradual and prolonged process, which hopefully goes on all the days of our lives. Of course, getting better provides more and more experiences in which we can employ our healthier selves and this in itself provides practice and growth and enhances the growing experience, thus establishing a healthy cycle. While we are here, let me also say this. Getting insight, getting better, never happens in a straight painless line. Getting better is like a fever curve—there are ups and downs. We take five steps forward, two steps back—five more steps forward, etc. There are bumps in the road— growing pains—but these are *growing* pains, concomitants to growth, rather than suffering for its own sake or for destructive purposes.

Insight and willpower

Willpower is often confused with insight and understanding. People feel that an enhancement of willpower or an act of willpower will be an ample substitute for insight. They feel that all you have to do to be better at relating is to be told how to do it (as if there were a simple formula) and then to simply use ample willpower to get it done. Well, willpower can be a valuable commodity, but it will only be useful if used in conjunction with insight. People who are in great emotional trouble suffer great pain and they would do anything to get well. Many have ample willpower. If this were all that was necessary, we could empty the overcrowded state mental hospitals overnight. But only insight can extricate a human being from a long-standing emotional morass for a prolonged period of time. One cannot free himself from disastrous emotional entanglements and self-destructive enterprises unless he knows how and what they are all about and how and what makes for his involvement in them.

Willpower as a pure act invariably comes from compulsive drives and contracts and further contributes to compulsion. There is no real *self* involved in an attempt to overwhelm a disastrous situation by an act of "strength" alone. It just doesn't work. Insight, on the other hand, involves real knowing of self and real self-involvement on the deepest level. This means that the problem is fully understood on a feeling level through a careful, detailed working through. The crucial issue in insight is what a person feels (feels/knows) rather than what he thinks. Let me give you an example—a vastly oversimplified one, perhaps—but I think it will make the point. You can think about chow mein and all of its ingredients, you can "know" the chemistry of the ingredients in detail. You can talk about it to the point of exhaustion, *but* you will not *know* the taste of chow mein with your feelings until you eat chow mein. Eating it will be the real knowing of chow mein and will give you a knowing memory that you will not soon forget. Insight is akin to that kind of knowing—the knowing that comes from tasting, chewing, swallowing and digesting.

Now why is insight such a formidable tool in establishing reality, in making problems solvable and in enhancing growth and better relating to Max? The fact is that deep down (no matter how people may seem to cling to suffering on the surface) people all want to be well and to be happy. However, they cannot willpower themselves out of a problem when they know nothing about the whats and hows of that problem or group of problems. Insight is the key that can free them. Let me give you another very simplified but pertinent example. Let us say that Sam has a very severe allergy to tomatoes. Each time he eats tomatoes he gets violently ill, even close to death. Let us say that he would do anything not to get sick and undergo the terrible suffering brought on by his allergy. However, Sam does not know that he is allergic to tomatoes. He doesn't even know that he has any allergy at all. He attempts to will away his symptoms with all kinds of inappropriate stratagems. He wills himself to get more rest. He does not permit himself too much exercise and so on. None of these works because his basic problem continues to be unknown and therefore continues uninterrupted. When Sam finally, after much examining, testing and careful investigation, finds out that his reaction (what) is an allergic reaction, he is well on his way to getting better. He then finds out that the allergy is to tomatoes and is told how he reacts and what to do. He is told to take an antihistamine any time he suspects that he has unwittingly eaten tomato in a sauce, and of course to avoid tomatoes whenever possible. Since Sam wants to be well, since he now knows how to be well, since he now has *insight*, it is very easy for him to exert willpower constructively, and he does so in his avoidance of tomatoes and keeping well. His knowing about this allergy is not on a purely thinking or intellectual level by any means. The fact is that he has gone through (as a whole person) all of the pain, suffering, investigating and testing necessary to a solution. He was there and he participated in his own problem. It was no mere act of willpower.

Let me give you another example from my own practice experience—and a very common problem. I had a patient who for years engaged in a sado-masochistic relationship with her husband (not unlike the principal characters in *Who's Afraid of Virginia Woolf?*). He was the sadist, she the masochist. He was mean, arrogant and vindictive to her and she stayed on and absorbed the pain as part of a martyred resignation. As an initial reaction to her treatment and to her feelings of support from me, and some newfound self-esteem, she made up her mind to do something about it. Again and again, as an act of willpower, she fought back and "told her husband off," only to very quickly slip back into her role of "victim" each time. After considerable time and work, she developed a real insight into her difficulty. Her problem and his was complicated and multifaceted and I am only describing one aspect here, but a very important one that made life more tolerable. I say "developed" because her insight did not occur with a flashlike suddenness. A thinking/knowing occurred in a seeming flash illumination to her (actually after much more work on both our parts than she was aware of) and she at first mistook it for the real thing. But knowing, really knowing, feel/knowing took months. It only occurred as a slow emotional development and as a result of great work. This insight consisted of the fact that she goaded, provoked and manipulated her husband into victimizing her. She was as absolutely involved in each of her martyred experiences as he was. This was covered over by great protestations of suffering and need for succor—and she did indeed, suffer. The fact is that her need to suffer and her need to get relief were not mutually exclusive. They were both there and going on at the same time. She "saw" all this relatively early in the game, but seeing this on an emotional—that is, on an insightful—level took much longer. She had to see and feel how she had done this for years. She had to learn that part of her attraction to her husband was based on this need. She had to "see" and "feel" how and where this need started and developed; and how it fit in with other aspects of her behavior. Then she had to see *how* she attempted to do the same thing with me. *How* her suffering for martyred glory was, in fact, a poor substitute for real aliveness. *How* she sabotaged herself with it. When she finally became aware—really aware—and dared to enter into an unfamiliar kind of behavior, it took very little willpower to extricate herself from this disastrous enterprise and to refuse to contribute further to it in any way. Fortunately her husband had also been in treatment for some time and together they were able to construct a really fruitful relationship. Needless to say, this could never have happened as an act of willpower. Such an act would have been superficial, paltry and fleeting, compared to what was really needed, namely, insight, emotional knowing on the deepest level, emotional working through, and understanding of what, when and how.

Goals I and II

(I) Working for greater health, happiness and success in relating and (II) working to make your neurosis work and to be a more successful neurotic. Of course, the difference is vast and the issue is urgent: (I) makes for a constructive use of energy; (II) couldn't be more destructive. Yet the two are constantly confused. This is not hard to understand when we realize that there are many, many people who have no idea that they have been functioning and relating in a sick way or that a change and greater success are possible. Sickness becomes a familiar way of life and people not only cling to the familiar, but soon forget that a time existed when things were "different." I have seen people who have been afraid of trains, cars, tunnels, etc., for many years, who take it for granted that this is the way it has to be and that no change is possible. I have seen other people and in fairly large numbers, who have been depressed for so many years that they have forgotten what it feels like to feel good and have no idea that they are depressed. Yet their depression is evident to me in the way they talk, eat and generally function. Their depression becomes apparent to them when they begin to feel good for the first time in years (in treatment). Feeling good is such a contrast to how they have been feeling for years that at first, this "new" feeling is strange and unfamiliar. They then become aware that they have been functioning with only a fraction of their potential for success and happiness for years. Every practicing psychoanalyst can tell you that his patients' goals are initially far different from his own. The patient wants the analyst to help him make his neurosis work. The analyst wants the patient to give up his contractual compulsive behavior in favor of healthy spontaneity. The patient wants to find out how to change the environment to fit in with his neurotic needs. The analyst wants the patient to change himself by growing more mature and realistic so that he is better able to cope with the existing environment. The patient to whom mastery has always been most important wants the analyst to help him to subdue the world, so that his mastery will work. The self-effacing, compliant patient wants her doctor to help her to be loved by everybody in her world. The detached person wants to know how to function better with less and less involvement, off on cloud 9. I remember a patient who was a prostitute and who had been in jail a great many times. When I questioned her, she told me that she didn't want me to help her to give up prostitution. She really hoped that treatment would help her to be a more successful prostitute and to be able to spot policemen so that she could stay out of jail. To be more successful at rigid and compulsive behavior invariably has very serious repercussions in relating to Max. To become healthier means to become more flexible and open, which invariably makes better relating a possibility. But more about openness later on.

Feeling lovable and narcissism

Narcissism is sometimes confused with "self-love." Narcissism is not self-love. It is compulsive preoccupation with self to the exclusion of all others and all else. If it is severe enough, the individual feels cut off from the rest of the world and solitarily encapsulated and separated from all that goes on outside of himself. We see lesser forms constantly and to a certain extent, we are all narcissistic. There are various manifestations: people who spend inappropriate amounts of time at the mirror and beauty parlor; overconcern with dressing; great efforts made at getting admiration. Of course, many people like to look well. But there is a difference between liking to look well and a compulsive preoccupation with one's appearance. Great narcissism is a very complicated disorder and a thorough discussion does not concern us here. But on one level, what are these people looking for? They are looking for reassurance to mitigate their own feelings of unlovability and self-hate. So narcissistic, exclusively self-interested people feel anything but lovable. People who feel lovable may enjoy admiration, but they don't *need* it and are not devastated when they don't get it. These are people who are self-accepting and who like themselves enough (they have considerable self-esteem and own their assets) so that they want to and can share themselves with others. They are sufficiently convinced of their worth without spending great time and energy in a seclusive attempt to give false self-esteem. They can share themselves with others because they feel that there is enough of themselves to share without being depleted.

Grandiosity and ownership

Owning what you've got and grandiosity are not interchangeable things. Owning what you've got is *not* grandiosity. Grandiosity is, as a matter of fact, a reaction to non-ownership. Bragging and acting the big shot are actually attempts to convince one's self of ownership that is not felt. A real owner does not have to act in the grand manner. He knows who he is and what he's got, and does not need other people's reaction to him or reassurance in the form of admiration to convince him of ownership. He also does not have to act modest—really another form of getting a needed reaction of admiration and approval. He knows what he is and uses what he's got without false modesty and without bravado.

In our society, there is very often a fear of grandiose behavior and its implications, to the point of hiding what one really has and what he knows that he has. This can be a very destructive enterprise, especially when Max is a co-worker, colleague or superior on the job. I, for one, believe that it is often quite destructive to keep one's assets and skills a too closely guarded secret. You needn't fear that it will seem like you are bragging. If you really own what you've got and are not attempting to falsely impress and to manipulate Max into making statements of admiration, you will come across exactly as what you are, namely—a self-confident person who knows what he's got.

Pain and pain

I just want to say here that emotional pain does not always come from the same sources or serve the same masters.

There is pain that comes of giving up old, sick, but familiar patterns of behavior. Again, this can be the pain of growing, born of taking a chance for the sake of better relating and eventual greater happiness. This is like the pain inflicted by any doctor or dentist in the process of getting well. This is not pain for pain's sake, but rather an unavoidable concomitant of growth in a healthy direction.

The source of neurotic suffering and pain can be so complicated and convoluted that it is impossible to tell where it is coming from, let alone what it is all about and

where it is going. Very often, the pain in neurotic suffering is, in itself, the main product and purpose—that
is, pain for pain's sake. There are people who cannot feel
at all, who, in fact, feel quite dead unless they are in
pain. Pain is the only emotional sensation they are aware
of and react to and thus much of their life's energy is
spent in seeking it. This masochistic activity takes
many forms, some blatant and some subtle. Some of
these people always manage to be in financial difficulties, in legal trouble, taking drugs, in accidents, in all
kinds of destructive self-punitive relationships, etc. Then
of course, there are those people who seek "to endure"
pain, for the sake of martyrdom and glory through martyrdom. Many of these people use their suffering as a very
potent instrument of manipulation against unknowing
victims ("I am in such pain—how can you leave me?" "If
you get angry at me, I'll get one of my severe sick headaches." "I've been terribly depressed since you told me
you want to go into business for yourself." "Don't you
even consider the pain you are causing me," etc., etc.) Of
course, much neurotic pain is the result of completely
unconscious forces. The individual is in pain, but has no
real knowledge that he is instrumental in producing it—
let alone where it comes from or what purpose it serves.
Self-hate in the form of depression (and there is little
in life that can be more painful than the suffering of a
severe depression) is a very common form of pain brought
on by self-chastisement—self-berating—in which the
victim is unaware of his own participation in the act
(knowing—real emotional knowing of his self-hate and
self-execution—judge, jury, executioner—often relieves
the depression very effectively). In any case, neurotic
pain or suffering is part and parcel of a destructive process which in no way enhances healthy growth or success.
    Let me close discussion of this muddle with one other

observation. Suffering as a concomitant of healthy growth (growing pains), as well as suffering endured through no choice or design of our own making, almost always evokes sympathy. Neurotic suffering often evokes disgust and contempt. This is largely so because neurotic suffering is perceived by Max as a waste, as destructive, as always being there and never going anywhere. This kind of suffering blots out the individual's other assets to such an extent that he becomes a terrible bore, a kill-joy, a promoter of failure and hopelessness. Max soon realizes (sometimes unconsciously) that this suffering is used as a manipulative tool and he does not care to be manipulated. It is easy to see how neurotic suffering eventually becomes exceedingly destructive to successful relating to self and to others.

Anger and anger

Volumes could be written describing the confusions that are prevalent about this most common human emotion. In a later section, I will discuss anger and its proper handling in relating to Max. Let us here try to clear up a few of the most prevalent (and destructive) confusions.

Anger does not kill. This statement sounds obvious, but a great many people believe that anger kills. Many of them don't know that they have this belief. It remains unconscious and they remain unaware of it, but their handling of anger is governed by this belief. Well, anger doesn't kill even though angry people sometimes do. Those who do are very sick people and anger plays a very small role in their becoming killers. Anger itself (an outburst, yelling, words) will not kill or for that matter hurt anybody physically in any way. It is important that both you and your children know this. The object of your anger will survive very well. However, anger that is repressed *can kill* a relationship. When somebody is angry and hides it from himself, it can be quite self-destructive, both emotionally and physically. This is the stuff that gastrointestinal disturbances such as duodenal ulcers are made of. When you are angry and hide it from Max, a coldness usually develops—a sullenness—and a breakdown in communication. The gulf that develops becomes still wider since Max doesn't know that you are angry and has no chance to straighten out any slight hurt, etc., that he may have been involved in. Now this brings me to a very important aspect of anger. Anger, experienced and expressed between people, can be a warm emotion which is often followed by feelings of love. However, as mentioned above, anger can be other than warm or communicative. It can be a cold, sullen thing which is kept to one's self and which eventually may result in vindictive acts or inappropriate bursts of rage. Warm expressions of anger are indications of considerable health and a general ability to emote in all areas, including love. Cold repressed sullenness and vindictiveness are usually an indication of difficulty in relating emotions other than anger (particularly love). Let me say at this point that inappropriate or great anger is more often than not the result of hurt pride. In this connection, psychoanalytic treatment in revealing areas that are protected by pride, thus removing the need for neurotic pride and the possibility of hurt pride, also removes reactions of disproportionate rage. But psychiatric treatment does not remove human reactions of warm anger, any more than it does any other basic emotion; any more than it removes any reflex reaction like, for example, the knee jerk.

Two more things: First, anger is not forever. Just as we said earlier, when a mother thinks or says "Drop dead" to a child, she doesn't mean forever—and she doesn't stay angry forever. None of us does. We get angry and it passes and is over. Yet, many people feel that their anger will last forever, or that the "devastation" caused by it will last forever, or that anger directed at them is forever. You can be angry at Max or Max can be angry at you. Expressed with zest, it will pass and leave both of you closer and in good condition. Secondly, an expression of anger, a temper tantrum, is not a sign of lunacy. This, too, sounds obvious, but many, many people regard an angry reaction on their parts as sure evidence of insanity. This is especially so of people who have great pride invested in being liked and who view anger as a threat to being liked. It is also true of people who have great pride invested in mastery of their emotions. An angry outburst is seen as a loss of emotional control and as going berserk. Actually, it may be a sign of loosening up, becoming more human, and the beginnings of greater health and better relating.

"I feel." I should feel and therefore I do feel

This is a very common one. But there is an enormous difference between the two. "I feel" refers to really feeling and to feeling any way, regardless of acceptability or expedience concerning the feeling. This is especially applicable in your feelings about or toward

Max (especially when Max is a child, parent, wife or husband).

"I should feel and therefore I do feel" very often passes for the real thing. This one involves feeling the "right" feelings toward Max to the exclusion of all others. (Again, this is particularly applicable to one's children, parents, or spouse.) These are, of course, based on compulsive hidden contracts, in which the individual manufactures the "right" feelings (right according to his contract "learned" from society's often unrealistic demands, conventions and lessons).

The individual who does this is often completely unaware of the process and cannot differentiate a real feeling from a conveniently manufactured contracted one. One of the big clues to the difference is that the synthetic one is more often than not absolute, all-encompassing, and often contributes to the winged-back phenomenon (feeling like an angel). Some typical statements are: "A mother always loves her children," "I never get angry at my parents," "I've never been tempted in that way," "Making other people happy has always been my greatest source of enjoyment," "No! I guess I do like everybody. I just never get angry."

Decisions—making the right one

There is a big difference between decisions arrived at through logic and decisions arrived at through feelings. Of course, there are decisions which must be arrived at through intellectual rationale—e.g., an accountant figuring out a client's total estate and tax picture.

Though even here as in all such cases, feelings will (sometimes inadvertently) have their effect. But I am talking about decisions concerning one's feelings, values and principles. These decisions concern some very important issues, e.g., marriage, divorce, choice of career, etc. Very often, these decisions are arrived at through logical rationale and reasoning, and as an act of willpower. This passes for decisions based on feelings, and though logic and feelings are not mutually exclusive (both can go on at the same time), very often such decisions unfortunately have nothing at all to do with what the individual feels. The fact is that the person may not have ever consulted his feelings at all. He did not give himself a chance to feel. This is especially true of people who are afraid to feel, who put down feelings and whose total pride is invested in their ability to be logical. These people will spend hours "figuring the thing out" before they decide what to feel and how to feel. They will then tell themselves that they do feel and they will make a decision and act on it. Some of these decisions are disastrous indeed, because they are not based on what the particular person feels at all. This is especially true in choices involving Max (marriage, job, etc.). When a decision is based on feeling—on really knowing—with the core of one's feelings and one's self, it is truly fascinating how quickly made and how right that decision feels. It is also interesting that it takes enormous twisting and rationalizing to twist this emotional decision into an opposing "logical" decision, which may for one or another reason be more in keeping with conventional needs.

Nathan Freeman used to say, "In times of important deciding, listen to your belly button." What he meant was to listen to our guts as to what we really felt, to the inner core of us. This is not to be confused with an impulsive decision. A "belly button" decision can take time, but given the time and sufficient *self* and contact with self, it will come through.

"*I was never sick before*"

This statement and others like it ("I never had this problem before") indicates confusion about sickness or emotional disturbance or having emotional difficulties or problems. This statement is another way of saying, "How can that be? Impossible? But I never had it before." In other words, it is a form of denial or an attempt at evasion of a problem by the spurious rationalization that "If I never had it before, I can't possibly have it now." Let us apply this logic to pneumonia—I may never have had pneumonia (or measles) before, but if I've got it now, I've got it, and I'd better do something about it if I want to get well—and live. Not only does this apply to emotional difficulties, but there is usually another factor as well. When an individual says he was never sick before (emotionally), he almost always means that he never had symptoms (depression, phobias, severe anxieties) before or is not aware of ever having had them. *But* chances are that he has in fact had serious problems of personality and relating, long before he developed symptoms, which, like measles, he never had before. There is even a chance that he has had subtle manifestations of symptoms, too, which up to a point he was able to put aside.

Most people have some personality problems, that is, poor ways of handling feelings and emotions and concomitant problems in relating. Most people don't know it

165

because their overwhelming health and assets permit them to function well. Some people have greater problems and are usually just as unaware as are their healthier confreres. When an impingement by the environment (e.g., business reversal or some area in which pride is sorely attacked) results in a break up of defenses and subsequent emotional pain in one or another forms, with some loss of function, they then feel that they are sick, for the first time, "never having been sick before." In actuality, they have been sick or have had problems for years. But this all went on, on a relatively "painless" level, even though there must have been a concomitant (often unconscious) ill effect on relating and functioning. The "new" painful symptoms (depressions) may be there for the first time, but would not be possible at all if long-standing problems did not exist.

The fear of pleasure

Pleasure and seeking pleasure are to be regarded as potentially destructive and should be viewed with suspicion and caution. True or False? Most of us feel that seeking happiness is a perfectly okay pursuit. But you may be surprised to find out that there are many people who feel otherwise. Most of them are not aware that they suffer from this belief, but their actions indicate that this is only too true. These are people who somehow thwart and sabotage themselves, just when they are on the verge of any success. They are people who somehow get very little pleasure out of ordinarily pleasurable pursuits. These are people for whom happiness is always an elusive item. For them everything is too good. They somehow manage to live way below what they can afford or way above what they can afford (so that they are always under pressure). Many enforce a Spartan regime when it is uncalled for and unnecessary.

In reality they are afraid of pleasure and when engaged in pleasurable activity, they feel that they are breaking a contract. Following an unusually happy event or period, they often become very depressed and "sick" emotionally. The origin of this kind of muddle can be very complicated and obscure and is of course always individual. But, to a large extent, regardless of origin, it becomes a long-standing habit which is impossible to break unless the victim is aware of the trap he is in. I have known people caught in this muddle in whom the dynamics varied considerably. Let me just describe a few:

1) Helen came from a fanatically religious home where she was literally taught to regard all pleasure and unusual happiness as possible evidence of depravity and sin.

2) John came from a background where any show of feeling was considered weakness. This especially included laughter. This austere background produced a man who was frightened to ever let himself in on what he felt. This was especially true of pleasurable feelings which he saw as particular signs of weakness.

3) Betty came from an exceedingly perfectionistic background and simply felt that she didn't deserve any pleasure unless she fulfilled extraordinary requirements. Since this was impossible she unwittingly sabotaged her every effort at happiness. She distinctly remembered playing and laughing with her sister and her mother saying, "Laugh in the morning, then you will surely cry at night." On the few occasions when she permitted herself

particular pleasures (a vacation, buying a new home) she became very depressed and didn't know why. This eventually led to occasional feeble attempts at pleasure which were camouflaged by a sour, dour expression. When asked, she always (safely) managed to describe any successes of her husband and herself in such a way that it sounded more like tragedy. It was only after she became thoroughly aware of her contract for perfection that she was able to give up to a considerable extent this need to camouflage pleasure. This, plus the insight of how she functioned on an irrational reward and punishment basis, finally permitted her to be humanly pleasure-seeking and, incidentally, also saved her marriage (living with a chronic-sufferer can be excruciating torture indeed for a non-sufferer).

I desire—therefore, you owe me

Karen Horney calls this muddle a neurotic claim and describes it brilliantly in her various works. This is an extremely prevalent muddle and one of the most destructive to one's self and to relating to others.

In this one, a need may become a desire and then a desire is converted to a "legal claim." It goes like this: "I need $10,000 to go into business."——"I wish I had $10,000 to go into business"——"You have money."—— "You *should* give me $10,000 to go into business."—— "You owe me $10,000 to go into business."——"My not going into business is your fault."——"I hate you and my rage is entirely appropriate." Of course, this is a simplified example.

Let me give you an example of another claim from my own practice. My patient, a doctor, was an extremely shy and self-effacing man, so much so that he chose radiology as a specialty, since he would have minimum contact with people, though he actually preferred general practice. He was at a cocktail party with his wife. The guests sat around the periphery of a very large room. Drinks were placed on a table in the center of the room and guests helped themselves as they desired. However, my patient could not get up to serve himself—he was too shy to walk to the center of the room. His wife was not thirsty and didn't get up, either. After several hours of intense thirst, they left. On the way home, they were silent and he was sullen. After a few minutes, he suddenly pulled up to the curb and with great anger yelled at her, "You and your friends—at least they could serve a guy a drink!"

In actuality, they were not her friends but his hospital colleagues. In effect, he was saying, "I am too shy to get up; therefore, I desire them to serve me so that I don't have to get up. As a matter of fact, they owe me this service and not paying this debt they are no longer friends of mine. Since you didn't get up, they are like you and are therefore friends of yours. Besides which, I can't admit all this because it hurts my pride that I should be so helpless. Therefore, I take it out on you."

A claim converted from a desire can spring from any number or combination of issues, can be subtle or blatant, can have dozens of ramifications and can be beautifully rationalized. The individual making the "claim" has no idea that he is being irrational. He feels completely justified—"It is coming to me"—and invariably reacts to a refusal, or claim frustration, with great inappropriate anger, expressed or unexpressed or both. This kind of irrational reaction, if further complicated by envy and jealousy, destroys relationships and has an exceedingly corrosive effect on one's *self*. It makes for cynicism, bitterness and much waste of time and energy. It is clearly one thing to have a wish, but quite another to feel that a person or people owe us the debt of satisfying that wish. People who carry this muddle to vast proportions really feel that the world owes them everything. When the world does not give them everything, they feel angry, thwarted, bitter and usually go on refusing to take responsibility for not getting what they want. They stew in their juice and wait and wait for someone or everyone to recognize their hurt feelings and their claim for reparations (claims based on hurt feelings and suffering and martyrdom run rampant: "I suffer so, been depriving myself for years, so when will something great happen for me?"). Of course, this doesn't happen. People are busy living their lives and may be totally unaware of individuals in pain from suffering of their own making. Of course, the individual who is particularly trapped in this muddle not only feels hurt, vindictive, incapable of a sustained relationship (destroys them by inordinate demands on Max), incapable of pleasure, but also deprives himself of the responsibility necessary in attempting to fulfill his desires himself.

"You made me do it!"

"You made me feel guilty!" "You made me depressed!" "You put me in this mood." "I did it because you made me do it!"

Many people actually believe that other people made them do this or that or put them in this or that mood. Nobody, but nobody, can make you feel this or that. Nobody can make you feel guilty, etc. If you feel depressed because Max said something, did something, etc., it is you who are making yourself depressed, as a reaction to Max, but Max is not making you depressed.

Let us look at a fairly common statement: "So and so made a fool of me." Can anyone make a fool (or a wise man) of you? Of course not. You either are a fool or you aren't a fool or you feel like a fool or you don't feel like a fool. Nobody can make you a fool, any more than anybody can make you a doctor. They can give you the books, the instruction, but you must make a doctor of yourself. *But* you can use what someone says to make yourself feel like a fool. This comes with special ease to those who have poor self-esteem and who are always terribly concerned with what other people think, and who are also terribly suggestible.

It is extremely important to clarify this issue. Putting responsibility for how we feel or act outside ourselves deprives us of the possibility of governing our own lives. This makes each of us a will-o'-the-wisp, subject to the moods, words, and decisions of other people. This would mean that in order to change our particular situation, feeling, status, etc., we would have to change another person or persons with whom we come in contact. Fortunately, this is not so. We only have to change ourselves, a completely possible task. But in order to do this, we must take responsibility for ourselves. We can take that responsibility only if we realize that we may react to other people, but that *we* are doing the reacting. *They are not making us do or feel anything.*

I have heard parents say, "For the last twenty years I have lived only for and because of you." If a parent has lived only for you, then remember this is not your doing. It was his or her choice, not yours. You did not make them "live only because of you." You owe them nothing special for this. You still very much desire to live your own life. This "last twenty years" kind of statement is based on this muddle and is designed to manipulate by generating guilt. It is a terrible burden to put on a young child who, in his innocence, feels that he not only now has responsibility for his own life, but also the crushing responsibility of his parent's life as well.

A friend of mine is a psychoanalyst. He told me that a patient came to him for a consultation and in their first session the patient said, "Doctor, I'm putting my life in your hands. Just take over for me." Whereupon my friend threw up his hands and replied, "Oh, no! I have enough to do living my life without taking over yours." He went on to add that he would help the patient resolve problems so that he would be better equipped to live his own life with greater success. Of course, what he said, in effect, was that each of us lives his own life and is responsible for it and that nobody makes you do anything. If you feel that someone is making you do something, chances are you are using that someone "to make you do what you want to do," unless you simply can't say no to anyone's pressure. But the problem, whatever it is, is yours, and this is good because it means that the possibility of resolving it is also yours and therefore can be done.

Self-consciousness and self

Consciousness of self is sometimes confused with feeling for self, that is, with having a strong sense of self and identity. No such thing is true. When one is truly one's self, he is least aware of himself. He is too much involved in being himself to be viewing himself as if from

172

outside. He *is* himself and in the process of being himself he isn't split into two people, one of whom stands outside and views the other. Great consciousness of self is just that: the individual is separated from his true identity and sees himself as having a special awareness or overburdening consciousness. This overemphasized awareness is only possible when there is great separation between an individual and what he really is (his *self:* comprising his values, feelings, etc.). In any case, I will have much more to say about the all-important item called "self" in a later section.

Sado-masculinity and maso-femininity

Sadism is strength and a male characteristic. Masochism is weakness and a female characteristic. Not so! This muddle is really a part of the male/female muddle, but it is so common and so destructive that I feel it deserves mention as a separate entity. There are still orthodox Freudian analysts who not only believe that this is true, but who also believe that sadism and masochism (satisfaction in inflicting pain or suffering, and satisfaction in receiving pain or suffering) are inborn characteristics of all people. Many analysts, including myself, do not believe this at all. We believe that sadism and masochism and any form of compulsive cruelty, given or received, are part and parcel of complicated emotional disturbances and can be remedied. I have seen any number of men and women who suffer from sadistic and masochistic tendencies and indeed, if one is present the

173

other isn't far behind. In sado-masochistic relationships between two people, the roles are switched very often. If men seem more sadistic and women more masochistic, it is only because they feel that these are culturally acceptable roles. That is because they see one as masculine and the other as feminine when, in fact, neither is the exclusive province of either sex and both are characteristic of emotional disturbance in both sexes. Sadism and masochism, of course, are never evidence of strength. Rather, they are evidence of feelings of deadness and emptiness and an attempt at feeling alive through the stimulating effects of feeling pain—in others and in one's self. People who have the confused idea that a particularly vicious person is strong and reliable, more often than not will be bitterly disappointed should they have need to rely on that strength.

Safe and unsafe

This one is an offshoot of the familiar-unfamiliar muddle, but I feel it is important enough to discuss in its own context.

Of course most of us have realistic feelings and come to logical conclusions about what is safe and unsafe. This very valuable ability plays a crucial role in keeping us alive. But there is also a muddle here that is not relative to the foregoing. Quite often, without awareness, we come to feel that perfectly safe ventures, feelings, explorations, relationships, etc., are unsafe, only because they are unfamiliar or different and because we haven't experienced them. Very often we will stick with something truly destructive and unsafe only because it is familiar, because we have experienced it; it represents a status quo—no taking-a-chance situation. A good example of this on a very broad and national level was France's Maginot Line in World War II. France, familiar with forts and powerful fortifications throughout her long history, continued to rely on the "safe" familiar solution. She built the strongest line of fortification between herself and Germany ever built in the world. She did not investigate other possibilities or the changes necessitated by the modern world and its only too terrible destructive inventions. Relying on her concept of status quo safety turned out to be a complete fiasco. The Maginot Line was a complete failure—overrun and outflanked by the enemy's Panzer forces almost as soon as Germany decided to invade.

This kind of clinging to the "true and tested" can sometimes be of value if a particular situation is truly investigated and not bogged down by "what is safe is only that which is familiar." Otherwise, the "true and tested" can be a disastrously inhibiting and paralyzing trap that kills off potentially successful relationships before they ever begin. "I can't do it any other way" only too often means "I haven't done it any other way." To the compulsively self-effacing person, this may mean saying, "No!"—or simply asserting himself in any way. To the compulsively masterful person this may mean letting go of the reins. To the compulsively detached person this may mean getting involved. Any of these may represent taking a chance, but it will be a chance taken in the service of growth. More about taking a chance in a later section.

SECTION III

Sex Muddles

I have decided to discuss sex muddles in a separate section because they have much in common and because they are at once so prevalent and so destructive.

Sex offers the possibility of the closest kind of mature relating through physical closeness and fulfillment. It can enhance self-acceptance and self-esteem. Yet many people have unfulfilled and even tragic sexual lives. This is so for several reasons. *First,* and primary, is the fact that sexual activity between two people, in large measure, mirrors their entire relating experience. People who relate superficially cannot have a profound sustained sexual experience (this does not exclude the possibility of momentary mutual physical satisfaction). People who have personality and relating problems will usually also suffer repercussions in their sexual lives. *Secondly,* people have many muddled concepts about sex. These greatly attenuate their sexual possibilities and also contribute to poor relating in general, thus completing a vicious cycle.

When you give yourself to Max and I don't mean compulsively or neurotically, but out of free choice with a full heart, then an exchange always takes place. Max always gives himself (or herself) to you and you are both richer and replenished and have better selves for having made this emotional exchange. This to me is relating in a nutshell—the interchange of selves, the flow and investment of emotionale up and back. This is the stuff human beings thrive on. Without it, they die an emotional death. Now, sex can be the quintessence of this give-and-take or it can be a purely mechanical, physiological function. Of course this will depend on the feelings the partners have for each other, their emotional investments, and how free they are to express themselves in their sexual

179

interchange. Perversions in sex are relatively rare. However, there is much perversion *of* sex. This occurs each time potential beauty is converted to fear, ignorance and muddled anxiety.

The most common sexual confusions concern us in this section. Most of them occur in the form of misinformation and so-called truisms that simply are not true. Our job here is to debunk them once and for all. In this way, we can make for better sex activity and thus for better relating. In making for better relating, we make for better sex—thus establishing a healthy cycle.

Sexologists, experts, marriage manuals

There are bogus experts in the thousands who have written books, given lectures and have even set up offices for consultations. "Let the Buyer Beware." A fancy title (sexologist), a fancy office, the lecture platform and the printed word do not confirm expertise. The fact is, the vast majority of these "experts" are phonies and dangerous. They give much misinformation and very often their money-making goal is achieved through titillation rather than education. I am not against titillation, but misinformation can cause vast misery. Through the ages and particularly in the last twenty-five years, these nonexpert experts have contributed enormously to the vast storehouse of sexual muddles. Along with intentional and blatant chicanery and charlatanism, we have so-called nonprofit experts, who are not expert at all, but like other *analyzers* will render expertise at the drop of a hat. There are also those people whom the public inadvertently look upon as experts, often without the "expert's" awareness.

Many victims unfortunately come to believe that people involved in the entertainment industry (including novelists, actors, directors, screenwriters, etc.) are experts in understanding and explaining, either indirectly or by example, the complicated mechanisms involved in human sexual relationships. These people, as well as columnists and even writers of considerable distinction have done much to promote the confusion already in existence. It is a good idea to remember that the primary aim of entertainers is to entertain. Educational values, and especially education in sex, must be assessed carefully before being swallowed wholesale. A crucial part of that assessment is an evaluation of the source of knowledge. Let me warn you also that neither prostitutes nor professors are necessarily sex experts. They may have little else in common, but again and again I have heard members of both groups quoted as sex experts. As the former chief psychiatrist of the Women's House of Detention in New York City, I interviewed scores of prostitutes. Many told me of "Johns" who asked for their sexual advice, which they readily gave (such advice has also been published in books written by prostitutes). Well, let me say that of all the consultations I have had with people from all walks of life, I have never run into as much sexual confusion and sexual difficulties as I did with prostitutes. This group is made up of individuals with individual characteristics and problems. *But* one of the few generalizations I can make in psychiatry (with relative safety) can be made here. For all her sexualizing, the prostitute is almost always terribly confused about her sexual identification, about men, sex, sexual information, etc., and almost completely disassociates sex and relatedness. Her fund of misinformation concerning sex is usually staggering in its infantile naïveté. The same is not necessarily true of professors or academicians, but here, too, there are few experts. Again and again, I have heard students quote their teachers and professors in sexual matters. Unfortunately, these professors were professors of English, physics, engineering, etc. With all due respect to them as experts in their respective fields, they were not experts in either human physiology or psychology and they, too, contributed their share of muddles to the existing overburdened load.

What or who is a "safe" expert? Since sex involves the total human being, the expert is the man who is interested in this area and who is trained in terms of whole human beings. We must include human physiology, in all its ramifications, and psychology. At the risk of being accused of prejudice or having a vested interest, I still must say that the psychiatrist has the unique opportunity via his training to integrate or combine these various aspects of the human condition. He is trained as a medical doctor in all aspects of human physiology and its ramifications and has spent years in the study (and practice) of human behavior. Sex is a function of both; indeed, there is no dichotomy and the practicing psychiatrist knows this. He is well aware of sex as part and parcel of the general relating activity of human beings. He can never see a marriage manual, however explicit the directions, as a road map to sexual happiness since he knows that sex and emotions and relative maturity are inextricably interwoven. I must say that the best "sexologists" that I have met have been psychiatrists specializing in the area of marriage problems. Of course they functioned on a much deeper level than "marriage counselors." All right then, what about marriage manuals? Do they have any value? Of course they do—that is, good ones do. They are not panaceas. They don't tell you how to invest emotions. But they serve the very important function of providing a necessary knowledge of sexual physiology and technique. As such, they are invaluable and can contribute consid-

182

erably to dispelling muddles. I want to mention only one here, which I believe combines the very best that a marriage manual has to offer with one of the more glaring "faults."

Dr. Van de Velde's *Ideal Marriage* offers a superb education in sexual anatomy, physiology and technique. But implicit in the title and subtly implied throughout the book is the idea that marriage (here sexual union) can be and even should be ideal. This has been a basic fault and danger of marriage manuals, articles and lectures. This brings us to the next sex muddle.

The "ideal sex" muddle

There is little that is more destructive than the compulsion to have perfect or ideal sexual harmony. Any preaching, writing, lectures or teaching that contributes to this concept is enhancing a most destructive enterprise. Again and again, I see people in consultations, full of fear and trepidation, who have the misguided notion that their marriage is a failure. These people are actually under the impression that most other people enjoy a more (if not completely) perfect sexual harmony and that they themselves are therefore grossly incompatible and inadequate. Most often, neither is true, but they are so traumatized and shattered about unrealistic shortcomings (compared with what they think they ought to be) that they become severely inhibited and even sexually paralyzed. This further adds to the existing "evidence" and serves to make them feel even more inadequate and disparate. Many young couples are befuddled

183

by ancient sexual bugaboos, gleaned from "experts" and their publications, which would have them believe that sex must always be 100,000 percent intense, must always be as intense and glorious for her as for him, and must always be capped by an enormous number of enormous orgasms. All this must take place using prescribed methods only. If "other" methods are used, then it doesn't count. Besides that, "other" methods may even indicate some evidence of perversion and certainly point to lack of perfection.

Lack of perfection is interpreted as complete and utter hopeless and endless sexual inadequacy and incompatibility. Of course, all this is patent nonsense. But nonsense or not, it is extremely demoralizing to those people who are victimized by their respect for the "wrong" printed words. Let me say at once that if a young couple are relating in a give-and-take exchange of emotional energy (or caring), there is very little that they can find to do in sex that is "wrong," as long as it is not physically destructive (e.g., inflicting sadistic maiming of any kind). How can there be an ideal sexual relationship? Who is to say what is ideal and why there should be any one standard? Much of this drive to perfectionism masks a desire to conform and to belong. But to belong to what? Why can't people have their own particular sexual rhythms and preferences? Well, fortunately they can and they do and they all fall into what we may call normal human behavior—that is, if we consider normal as meaning nonharmful. If we were freer about conveying sexual information about ourselves to each other, we would surely reveal that there are differences, but surprisingly few surprises. We would find that *no* couple has a perfect sexual relationship (whatever criteria we choose to satisfy concepts of "perfection"). How can there be an ideal sexual relationship when there is no such thing as an

184

ideal relationship in any area or in all other areas? How can there be ideal relationships when relating takes place between people and ideal people simply do not exist? The fact is that we are fortunate indeed when we can engage in a relatively healthy give-and-take relating process, in which we can communicate something of ourselves to each other.

Please remember that sexual attitudes are symbolic of all other ways of relating to people. The manner in which a person expresses himself sexually is often very much linked to much of his inner life. Even masturbating, which is a solitary type of relating, is nevertheless an example of relating to one's self or to a fantasy. We may expect as many variations in sexual activity as there are kinds of people and ways to relate. However, the one kind that you will never find—at least not on earth—is the perfect man or woman or the perfect sexual partner or perfect sexual relationship.

Sex and emotional closeness

Sex is not always closeness. As a matter of fact, it is very often used to guarantee noninvolvement and distance. Periodically, I see a woman in consultation who states that she is very affectionate, wants a close relationship and more than willingly enters into sexual relationships. She goes on to tell me that she encounters the same difficulty with man after man. Sex quickly becomes mechanical, boring and even a burdensome nonfulfilling effort. Even more important and interesting, she says that despite her sexual encounter, she always has the distinct feeling that she never really gets to know her sexual partner. What becomes evident very rapidly is that there is ample sex, but little or no emotional exchange or mutual concern or interest. Again and again, her relationships end with her feeling more empty and unfulfilled than ever and once again in search of the real Max. Now how does she search for Max, that is, for a warm human relationship? She does this by going to bed with any potential Max almost at once and thus once again generating a situation which cannot possibly lead to a Max relationship. Well, what gives here? Let us call our consulting patient Irene, and let me say right off that there are scores of Irenes, most of whom have no awareness that they engender the very situation they claim they abhor. There is also a little of Irene in many of us, on a hidden basis. Now, how does Irene *use* sex—and she does in fact use it. She uses it to preclude the possibility of a close relationship. Yes, she *says* that she wants a close, give-and-take relationship replete with affection and warmth, *but* what she *does* is much more important than what she says. Well, what does she in fact *do?* She jumps into bed as quickly as possible, making absolutely sure that no time whatsoever is spent in conversation or an exchange of feelings about things, people, or each other. Despite what she says, she does not want closeness and makes quite sure that she doesn't get it. She is probably deathly afraid of real involvement, but doesn't know this. She has a vested interest and pride invested in not showing this fear ("doesn't everybody want closeness?") and she covers it up with sex ("isn't sex a sign of closeness?"). So, sex for her is both a cover up for her real problem and also a way of sustaining her problem, that is, continuing to guarantee noninvolvement and noncloseness. She uses sex to block the getting to know each other process, which ordinarily of course takes time. She uses sex to make sure that she and her partner remain superficial acquaintances. She makes sure that their relationship remains limited to the sexual area and does not progress to an *investment of feeling in each other stage* (where one can get great joy, but can also suffer loss and hurt). In short, Irene and the many Irenes do not use sex to get close, to express closeness or to sustain closeness. She, in fact, uses sex to maintain and sustain emotional distance. In her conscious mind, in her awareness, she confuses physical closeness and emotional closeness.

Why Irene has this particular difficulty is highly individual and varied. She may be afraid of what Max will find, or she may feel so little sense of identity and self that she feels that she will be "swamped and absorbed" by a close relationship. There are many possibilities, *but* she will surely not get *close* to Max until she can take a chance at a crack at real closeness. To do this, she must initially stay out of bed long enough so that she and Max can get to know each other.

It is very rare that people get to "know" each other unless they do so to a considerable degree before a sexual encounter takes place.

Penis, potency, sterility and lovemaking

How little they have to do with each other and how often they are seen in all kinds of confused connections.

My anatomy professor started his lectures on the penis by stating, "The average size of the erected penis is just under six inches. My wife had to be satisfied with just five." Well, can a woman be satisfied with five? Yes! And with less and even less and still less because the penis actually has very little to do with satisfaction. As a matter of fact, sexual enjoyment for either partner is hardly related to penis size at all. So let me clarify this muddle with several direct statements:

1) Sex as a sustained gratifying experience is largely influenced by how two people feel about each other generally, how much they love each other.

2) Male sterility and male impotence are not the same thing. They may or may not exist together. Generally, they do not. Sterility is a condition in which there is a low or no sperm count, so that there are no sperm to fertilize the female ovum. This in no way affects the man as a sexual partner. Impotence is a condition which does in fact hamper sexual performance, but is not related to sperm count. Sperm from the impotent male can fertilize the female egg. Some impotent men cannot get erections. Some get erections, but can not maintain them for long. Most impotent men have very quick ejaculations, usually before the penis is inserted into the vagina so that the erection is gone before intercourse can take place. Sterility is almost always an organic or physical condition. Impotence is almost always due to psychological difficulty and as such is best treated by a competent psychiatrist.

3) A man with a small penis can be as active, less active, or more active than a man with a larger penis. His level of sexual interest will depend more on his psychological makeup than his physiology and is not related to penis size.

4) Penis size and male capacity for sexual enjoyment are not related.

5) Penis size and the ability to give a woman sexual pleasure and satisfaction are not related. The penis is still the best instrument to deliver the sperm to the egg

so that fertilization can take place. *But* it is not the best instrument available in the service of pleasure. It is easily surpassed by the finger and tongue. There is very little that can match continued, sustained and gentle clitoral stimulation in the female pleasure department.

6) The size of the flaccid (not erected) penis plays no role in sex. Most erected penises fall within centimeters of the same size.

7) The worry and fear and embarrassment of having a smaller than adequate or average penis is extremely prevalent in the male population. These feelings are seldom related to the size of the penis. They are often related to one's self-esteem. Attacks of self-doubt and lack of confidence (e.g., a business reversal in a man who has a great investment of pride in business success) are often followed by a concern about penis size and sometimes results in temporary impotence.

8) "Success" as a lover or the ability to gratify sexually is related to mutual feelings of the partners and to lovemaking technique, and has little or nothing to do with the size of the male sexual apparatus.

9) In an emotionally healthy male, sexual activity can go on for the duration of life, even though desire may become less frequent.

10) There are very few men who desire (or can have) intercourse (with ejaculations) several times an hour. For most men (not teen-agers, who may be particularly vigorous) intercourse once a day is a great deal. Intercourse two or three times a week is usually more than adequate for most men. Rhythms and frequencies will vary from individual to individual and there is no such thing as a "normal rate." A "good lover" is not necessarily a frequent lovemaker. He *is* a man who is attuned to his wife's needs and cares about giving her pleasure when she is receptive to it.

Who are the best lovers?

Are handsome, athletic, masculine-looking men really the best lovers? Not necessarily. There is no correlation between muscles and lovemaking ability. Many athletic men have diverted much of their sexual interest to athletic endeavors and are not as competent as their flabby brothers. "Musclemen," that is, men who are particularly addicted to body-building (weight lifters), are often too self-preoccupied to make good lovers. Many of them harbor profound feelings of inadequacy which make for complicated sex problems including a relative lack of sexual desire. Looks and lovers have little to do with each other. Some of the homeliest men make excellent lovers. The movies often picture handsome, debonair men, drink in hand, as great lovers. Let me say that a little alcohol is relaxing and can be helpful, but that more than a little can inhibit and even anesthetize and paralyze the male sexual apparatus. Anyway, certain prototypes of what is considered handsome can, of course, be sexually attractive. I am certainly not knocking the indefinable chemistry (sexual attraction) that goes on between people. But a good lover is a man who likes women and who is enough concerned about a woman's satisfaction to have properly educated himself in the sexual sphere. Of course, there is no substitute for inspiration born of love for a particular woman. In any case, a man's looks, build or body type or muscles or lack of them will in no way be a measure of his sexual vim, vigor or ability.

The beautiful people

Every culture dictates what is and isn't "beautiful," but, fortunately, this has nothing to do with sex appeal. The fact is that different types appeal to different people. There is no universal sexually appealing type in either sex and it is destructive to feel that one must be attracted to only that type proscribed by society. Whatever the type, however, or individual taste, I feel that sexual attraction is either there or not there almost at once. There are exceptions though, and therefore, if all other aspects of a relationship are "glowing," it does behoove one to wait a little while at least for the possibility of sexual awakening.

Bosoms, psychology, health, and vitality

Some of the culturally fed bugaboos here are:
Sexual response in women is in direct proportion to the size of the bosom.

Shapely, large-breasted women are never frigid.

Small-breasted women are not capable of full sexual response.

Sexual response and vitality are purely physical and have nothing to do with the psychological life of the individual in question.

Sexual response and vitality are purely psychological and have nothing to do with physical health and vitality.

191

Of course, all of these statements are patent nonsense. We live in a breast culture, and the breast and all that it symbolically represents is adored and worshipped. But facts are facts. The breasts are not usually erogenous zones. The nipples are. Regardless of the size of their breasts, the nipples in various women are usually the same size. Nipple size has little to do with their excitory ability. Large- and small-breasted women are capable of no, little, moderate or great response and desire. The only import of breast size and shape in sex is the male's conditioned response to a particular kind of breast.

A state of good physical health and general vitality is helpful, but an individual's general personality makeup, ability to relate and attitudes toward sex are extremely important. These will far outshadow one's physical condition and are invariably the areas requiring exploration and insight in coping with sexual problems.

What is universal about love?

Is there a universal, expert love technique which is guaranteed to excite all men and all women, like a universal love elixir? More nonsense and pity the lover who follows any plan, book in hand, like a builder of a model airplane. It is true that important anatomical and physiological facts and aspects of stimulating techniques can be learned from marriage manuals. *But* a spontaneous, letting-go feeling and expressing of feeling are invaluable. I might mention here that I have interviewed any number of women who complained that their husbands remained silent during lovemaking. Women like to hear words of endearment and so do men. Words and expressions which describe and indicate pleasure received are often more stimulating than the physical contact which elicits them. Others, however, prefer a wordless communication.

Of course, there is no "universal method"; as members of the same species we may have identical anatomical structures, but our experiences, tastes and needs vary. It behooves sexual partners to explore and communicate each other's needs and preferences for mutual satisfaction.

Who starts?

In sex as elsewhere should men always be the initiators and leaders, and should women always be passive and the followers?

First, be wary of all truisms and especially those that have the word "should" in them.

This one unfortunately is an old hangover from the Victorian era, which certainly had its share of repressed sexuality and consequent misery. The fact is that some men will be more or less aggressive or passive than other men and the same is true of women. It is also true that people have different moods, feel different ways at different times and will at times feel more like initiators than receivers and vice versa. With most happy couples, both pitch in and both become initiators and passive and active at various times.

Are fellatio and cunnilingus perversions?

If they are, then a large percentage of the population is perverse. The fact is that many married couples enjoy oral-genital contact. There is absolutely nothing wrong with it so long as guilt doesn't ensue. If guilt follows or there is great inhibition, then there is obviously conflict present that needs resolving.

Is one big orgasm better than multiple orgasms?

For some people, this is true. For others, it is just the reverse. There are any number of women who are completely satisfied with a single orgasm each time they make love. They are in no way less passionate, less responsive or lesser sexual beings than women who have several or many orgasms.

Are multiple orgasms better than one orgasm?

For some people, this is true. For others, it is just the reverse. There are women who have several orgasms (with short intervals) during each intercourse experience. These women prefer to have their clitoris

194

stimulated again and again several times and achieve orgasm each time. A short period of rest is necessary between orgasms; otherwise the clitoris will be irritated, jumpy and generally refractory to stimulation. These women are neither less nor more passionate than the single-orgasm women. They have no lesser nor greater capacity for being maturely loving and they are neither more nor less "satisfied" than the other group.

Are infertile women always frigid?

No, this is absolutely not true. There are frigid (nonresponsive) women who get pregnant at the drop of a hat. There are highly sexed women who cannot get pregnant no matter what. Frigidity is nearly always emotional in origin. Infertility is sometimes emotional in origin, but is most often rooted in physiological difficulties (e.g., infantile or underdeveloped uterus, closed fallopian tubes, etc.).

And then the world explodes!

The expectations people have of themselves in sex are often fantastic. They not only expect orgasms but orgasmic experiences that will result in world explosion, earth-moving (Ernest Hemingway perpetuated this one in For Whom the Bell Tolls) or at least window-shatter-

195

ing. I'm all for big powerful sexual reactions. Participating in the perpetuation of the human race and making a contribution to the future is no small matter. It is no accident that nature made coitus a monumental experience and well it ought to be. Basically, it still represents the most important activity of the organism, whatever the species, because without it there wouldn't be any species. So fanfare is fine—but what have we done with it? We have (many of us, anyway) come to expect ecstasy of cataclysmic and increasing proportions each and every time we make love—even if we make it several times a day (not uncommon during honeymoons). Well, it doesn't work that way! Sometimes it's stronger and sometimes it's weaker. Some people have great enjoyment and satisfaction without orgasms at all. There are no rules! If it feels good, that's fine. Seismographic observations and mental records and graphs are not appropriate here. Every sexual reaction need not be an overwhelming, thoroughly exhausting, paralyzing one and indeed few are. Intensity of reaction is not the measure of love, nor is it the measure of masculinity or femininity. We human beings often expect more of ourselves and living on this planet than the human condition provides. We often want experiences that are simply not forthcoming on Earth. We simply do not want to accept the everyday stuff of working, eating, resting, entertaining, etc., as enough. But that, plus a few other things, is all there is. And it's awfully good stuff. Eating a piece of bread and butter can be the greatest— if you don't have wild expectations beyond the scope of being a human being on Earth. This especially applies to sex. It can be fun and emotionally gratifying too in just about every phase—if you don't expect and demand fantastic superman–woman feats and reactions akin to universe explosions. Sometimes sex is exciting, sometimes it is quiet, sometimes it is very, very exciting, and it is all good—if you don't keep a scorecard—and no seismograph, please!

Is sexual incompatibility due to great organ disparity?

I never heard of a case. I have known people who were seemingly unable to satisfy each other or themselves. But this never had anything to do with the size or shape of their genitalia. It was just about always related to personality and relating problems and invariably linked to a breakdown in communications. With psychotherapy and repaired communications, many of them learned to be patient, learned good technique and—"sexual compatibility."

What's wrong with too much sexual activity? Will it result in early termination of sexual life?

I don't believe it. As a matter of fact, too little can result in early termination due to a kind of resigned loss of interest. There is no "too much" if you don't get compulsive (feel that you should do it so and so many times) and if you don't get tired. If it is too much—because you feel you should do it out of a kind of coerced force, then it can lead to boredom and temporary termination until free interest is rekindled.

197

Does masturbation only occur among young males?

This is absolute nonsense, but very widely believed. Boys, girls, men and women masturbate. They do so whenever the sexual urge gets too strong to tolerate and there is no satisfying sexual partner available. Masturbation is a universal human practice. It also occurs among married people—sometimes when they are separated or incapacitated or, occasionally, as a simple matter of urge and urgency.

Masturbation creates no sickness, future sexual difficulties or neurosis or psychosis. Misknowledge, confusion and guilt involving masturbation can of course be destructive. Masturbation itself can be valuable in bringing relief from sexual tension.

The widespread guilt felt about masturbating is further proof of how many of us don't fully own our own bodies—our own selves—let alone have the free choice about what we do with ourselves.

Let me give you a few "crazy" ones at this point

What makes them even crazier is how many of us "sort of believe them a little bit":

The size of the nose is directly related to the size of the genitalia or to sexual ability.

The size of the feet is directly related to the size of the genitalia or to sexual ability.

Married people should sleep in single beds only!

Married people should sleep in double beds only!

Intercourse during menstruation is perverse and unhealthy and should never take place even though both people desire it.

Homosexual people always dress in a distinctive way.

Too much sexual activity leads to mental illness.

Too little sexual activity leads to mental illness.

Blond women have greater sexual potential.

Red-headed women have the greatest sexual potential.

Hairy men are exceptionally virile.

An intensely feminine woman experiences instant, intense, multiple orgasms.

Pipe-smoking men make good sexual partners.

An orgasm is necessary for conception.

"Sexy dressers" are good in bed.

Women have less sexual drive than men.

"Normal" sex practices are the same for all people all over the world, and are not related to upbringing or culture.

People should have intercourse on a regular schedule.

People who practice homosexuality are physiologically and anatomically different from other people.

A woman always likes gentle behavior in bed.

A woman always likes rough behavior in bed.

An ejaculation is always an orgastic experience.

Love is equal to mutual orgasm.

A man should always be in the mood, ready and capable of satisfying his wife.

A woman should always be in the mood, ready and capable of satisfying her husband.

Orgasm is the only indication of sexual satisfaction and adequacy.

If a partner is not aroused at once, this invariably indicates either waning interest or waning sexual prowess, or both.

People in love are good lovers

Not necessarily so. There are people who are well-trained and experienced sex technicians who know nothing of love. There are people who are in love and terribly concerned for each other's welfare and satisfaction who are poorly trained in sexual techniques. It behooves lovers to learn the fundamentals of sexual techniques, so as to be able to demonstrate their love sexually, in a mutually satisfying way. Dr. Theodore Van de Velde certainly gives adequate information concerning the anatomy and physiology of sex as well as good descriptions of possible positions, etc., *but* it must be remembered that we all have human limitations. We cannot be in perfect harmony at all times. Our reactions vary from one time to another and while we may be in love, this does not mean that the earth will explode each time we make love.

Is sex always "just" sex?

No. When sex is an expression of love, it is a joyous and probably the most fulfilling human encounter of all. But sex is not always an expression of love—not even between lovers.

There are times when sexual activity is the result of strong physical need and when love is not particularly felt even though it may be present. People in love don't always feel in an exalted state of loving.

There are times when sex is used to quell anxiety, almost as a sedative to make one sleepy. It may be used to feel closeness and support and reassurance as well as to quell anxiety and feelings of inadequacy.

Sex is sometimes used to work off repressed anger of which one is not aware. Unfortunately, it is sometimes used as part and parcel of private wars, in which the partners tease and frustrate each other without the awareness that they both have a vested interest in actually sabotaging their sexual effort.

Should women always have orgasms in intercourse?

It is particularly gratifying when a woman can have an orgasm whenever she feels the need or so desires. But, there may be many times when she does not desire an orgasm, but does desire one for her husband. It may at times give her ample satisfaction to make love, have intercourse and provide orgasm for her husband.

While it may be true that women are just as sexually desirous as men, neither their sexual physiology nor their psychology is identical to that of men. Once a man has attained erection and there has been sexual play for a period of time, he almost always wants an ejaculation. Indeed, it often becomes very painful to hold it back, let alone to forget it. Once set in motion, the male apparatus has a reflex autonomy which is most difficult to deny.

Women, on the other hand, can have considerable sexual play without becoming desirous of orgasm or feeling any slight or frustration if they don't attain it.

I have seen many, many couples who have felt enormous guilt because they could not adjust their rhythmic needs so that they both always wanted and attained orgasm at the same time. I feel that if possible, both partners should be satisfied whenever possible. However, satisfaction is not always the same for both partners. I think it is entirely realistic to realize the following:

1) The greatest urgency exists in the partner who desires sex at a particular time. Therefore, whenever possible, that partner's desires must be met rather than the partner who doesn't want sex.

2) When both partners want sex to orgasm, neither partner's needs are to be neglected. This is the time when both partners ought to work toward orgasm for each other.

3) If one partner desires orgasm and the other doesn't, there is absolutely nothing wrong with granting this desire. On the contrary, this makes for sexual adjustment, harmony and compatibility.

If the husband wants orgasm and the wife doesn't, she can derive considerable satisfaction in satisfying a most urgent need.

If she wants orgasm and he is too tired to perform with his penis, there is nearly never a reason why he can't satisfy her either manually or lingually, depending on their individual preference.

Please remember that we are talking about lovers, not adversaries. We are talking about two people who are intimately concerned with each other's happiness and contentment. There will be times when these two people will have climactic experiences together and other times when they will have them separately. But they will always be involved, available and happy to provide the relief and joy that sex can bring.

Sex as a pacifier

"Never let the sun set on a lover's quarrel" or "Don't go to bed angry—have sex instead."

These are bad rules because they often lead to a contrived and false "peace." I'm all for lovers making up and lovers often make up and make love and that's just fine, if it's for real. But to force sex when you don't feel like it is not a good idea. Also, there are times when lovers are angry and when the anger simply takes several days to dissipate. It may also take several days to get to understand the misunderstanding and to come to *real* peace with each other. There is nothing wrong with sustained anger, provided two people love each other enough to want to understand the hows and whats of it, so that the lines of communication remain intact. However, sexual partners must be wary not to use sex as a manipulative tool or as a pride weapon in anger. They must not intentionally deprive the other member of sex, as punishment. This can have disastrous consequences. It is one thing to feel angry enough not to want sex. It is quite another thing to hold out as a consciously vindictive act. Don't do it! The wound that will remain when you cut off your nose will be in your own face.

What are the "normal and acceptable" ways?

Are there only certain positions for women during the sex act? Of course this is patent nonsense again. Any position that helps a woman achieve maximum satisfaction is an excellent position.

Remember—a man has orgasms easily. His physiology is such that he can have an ejaculation with minimum stimulation. A woman often requires much more. Her very presence provides the man with almost as much as he needs to ejaculate. His presence alone is seldom not enough. Therefore, any position that will enable him to "hold back a little" while she "lets go" is a good position.

The long wait

A man should be able to have intercourse without ejaculation for great periods of time. Nonsense! Most men have orgasms after a few minutes of vigorous vaginal in/out stimulation. It is therefore mandatory that the man does not allow excessive stimulation to occur to his penis while he stimulates his partner fully, prior to intercourse. *Because* once intercourse starts, they must both have orgasms in a few minutes *because* he surely will.

However, there are positions in which intercourse can take place with minimum penis stimulation, still allowing maximum clitoral stimulation. For example, the woman can "sit" on her husband's penis while he rubs her clitoris with his finger. When she is about to "come," they can both get active enough—in/out—so that they will both have orgasms.

Some couples are particularly ingenious at positioning and timing, especially after having been lovers for a period of years. Very often, either partner's orgasm is enough to kick off the other's. It is always safer for the woman to begin her orgasm first for obvious reasons. But some women can't begin until they feel their husbands beginning first.

So who asks?

Some manuals dictate a procedure for initiating or asking for sex to begin.

This is nonsense. The best asking is usually no asking, but beginning and doing. However, there is nothing wrong with asking. If a man has a need and his wife doesn't and he asks and she lies back and says, "I'm tired, but you go ahead," there is absolutely nothing wrong with doing just that. *But* this must not be the procedure if she desires more than that!

Also, "fatigue" must not be used as a chronic dodge to avoid involvement.

Clitoral confusion

Thank God for the clitoris because without it, things would be very difficult. But it never ceases to amaze me that we human beings have such a fine talent for confusing and killing anything related to pleasure or anything that may be a source of pleasure.

Many people unfortunately have strange ideas concerning the clitoris and its use. Some believe that the need for clitoral stimulation means that something is wrong with the woman. Others have the crazy notion that a "real" man should be able to satisfy his wife with minimal clitoral stimulation. Others believe there is a clitoral orgasm which is distinctly inferior to a vaginal orgasm and as such, something to be ashamed of. Well, the confusion about the clitoris goes on and on. This is no surprise; as I said before, throughout our history we always manage to look upon sources of pleasure with great suspicion and then manage to generate crippling confusion. Of course, sex has suffered greatly in this respect and the clitoris, and what to do with it, perhaps more than any other part of human anatomy. Indeed, there are some primitive cultures where the clitoris (and labia minora—also an extremely erogenous zone) is amputated very early in life.

Let's try to make a few clarifying statements. There are few or no nerve endings in the vagina, which is neither a source of pain nor intense pleasure. The penis in the vagina gives a sense of fullness and an all-important psychological effect, rather than the effect of intense physical pleasure born of stimulation to an erogenous zone of first magnitude (the history of masturbation in most women indicates stimulation of the clitoris—not the vagina).

The clitoris is the most exquisitely sensitive structure in human anatomy. But it must be stimulated in order for it to realize its potential. When the penis is in the vagina, unless it is a very unusually shaped penis indeed, it cannot rub up against the clitoris, too. An attempt to do both (in/out motion and clitoral stimulation) will result in the penis slipping out of the vagina and will accomplish little in either area. There are marriage manuals that recommend one or another position and motion to achieve in/out motion and clitoral stimulation at the same time (they recommend "riding high," etc.). However, this is very unrealistic, to say the least. The best way to stimulate the clitoris is either with 1) the penis outside of the vagina, 2) a finger or 3) the tongue. The finger (or tongue) is much more adept for this purpose than the penis. After ample finger stimulation has taken place, the psychological effect of in/out motion may be enough to bring on orgasm. Otherwise, it is entirely practical, realistic and sensible to continue digital stimulation to the clitoris during intercourse until orgasm takes place. Any number of positions will lend themselves to this possibility. Once orgasm has taken place, the clitoris goes through a refractory period during which more stimulation will be irritating, painful and will produce jumpiness. As I've already mentioned, after half a minute or so has passed some women will desire more stimulation and more orgasms. Some will be satisfied with one orgasm.

An orgasm is an orgasm, and the clitoris produces it. There is no vaginal-clitoral dichotomy. There are orgasms of different qualities, however. Here is what I mean. There are times when an orgasm is felt locally almost solely in the clitoris. There are times when the intense sensation is felt vaginally, too (with muscular contractions). There are other times when the woman can "let go"—when orgasm reaches such global proportions that it is felt all over, as a total body and psychic involvement. But, regardless of whether the orgasm is a local or global one, remember that it is best initiated by steady and prolonged clitoral stimulation. Incidentally, the man, too, may experience purely local effects of ejaculation in the penis or stronger or orgastic feelings in the penis or the total or global orgasm which starts in the penis, but is felt totally (in which one's whole being is involved).

Menopause mythology

There are many menopause myths, among them the following:

Menopause results in frigidity and termination of sex life.

Menopause brings on one or another form of insanity.

The degree of emotional upheaval brought on by menopause is inherited.

Menopause is inevitably followed by an immediate degeneration and atrophy of the female sexual apparatus.

Of course, none of these is true. Women who have been sexually "involved and active" prior to menopause go right on being active. Some become even more interested in sex once the fear of pregnancy and the need for contraception is over.

Menopause, or cessation of menses, is not a cause for emotional illness. There are people who suffer from severe emotional problems all their lives. These women may sometimes be affected by menopause, but even here, menopause is a precipitating cause rather than a deep

208

underlying cause. Many women become very anxious at menopause because they have come to expect all kinds of trouble and develop tremendous trepidation about this most natural process. Some very immature women feel menopause as a great blow to their vanity and see it as undeniable evidence of aging. This kind of blow to the pride can bring on serious depression. Women who have been emotionally healthy, and who have a healthy, mature emotional outlook about the menopause will at most suffer "hot flashes" and other physiological symptoms. These are generally handled most satisfactorily by a competent gynecologist.

True love and exclusivity

A happy marriage, including a good sexual relationship, renders one impervious to the attractions of all persons but one's mate. Not so. The habits and conditioning of a lifetime may be repressed, but are not shut off by any relationship, sexual or otherwise, however satisfying it may be. This is expecting too much of marriage and puts a burden on a relationship that would best be avoided. Love cannot be measured in terms of exclusivity of attraction. However, attraction and temptation need not lead to action. This will, in large part, be determined by the values and histories of the individuals involved and by their levels of health and maturity, as well as the success of their relationship.

The list of sexual confusions is forbidding, its variations are endless and the inevitable product is misery. These misconceptions are rooted both in our cultural patterns and in the neurotic development of the individual. Unfortunately, too many people keep a mental checklist in which frequency of intercourse, orgasms and the like are carefully tabulated. A whole system of prides and resentments has developed, based on these "values." Spontaneity has been replaced with a book of rules. Most difficulties are not due to physical disproportion, but rather to mental maladjustments. The size of the genitalia presents almost no problems when compared with compulsive investments of pride in economic status, in prestige and in self-idealization. Again, I feel most strongly that sexual difficulties cannot be credited with causing neuroses, but rather that neurotic difficulties almost invariably make themselves felt sexually. Again, difficulties in the sexual area are merely another example of an impaired relationship to other people and to one's self.

SECTION IV

Making It with Max

Making it with Max is the central core, theme and purpose of this book. Remember, Max is a boy friend, girl friend, wife, husband, boss, colleague, client, son, daughter, audience, patient and anybody else with whom you have or desire to have a relationship.

Making it with Max means having a successful, sustained relationship with him, her, them. A *winner* is making it with Max. A *loser* is not. So much for our glossary.

Making it with Max means better relating to you and to other people. Thus, making it can help you to be more successful in business, sex, socially and in life, generally. People can change! I have seen losers become winners. You can make it with Max, but remember, your active understanding and participation are crucial. There is no substitute for insight into one's assets and limitations and into possible pitfalls and constructive possibilities.

To be a contest winner or to make it with Max

There are some teen-agers who are very popular and go on to become chronic contest winners. Unfortunately, many popularity contest winners become chronic losers. To make it popularly, more often than not, is the antithesis of making it with Max. Max is not looking for the most popular girl, boy, wife, husband, employee, colleague. He wants to make it with somebody who is not making it with the mob. To make it big in the big popularity contest too often means to be many things to many people. You must turn off parts of yourself to please some

213

people, turn on parts to please others, act this way, act that way, all in the quest of popular approval and admiration. This kind of self-fragmentation and acting does not present enough of one's true identity for Max to respond to or to even come in contact with. This precludes the possibility of involvement. Max simply cannot invest much emotion in fragments nor will he make any long-term commitments to someone who isn't quite there. The popularity contest entrant is busy reflecting the needs of her imagined judges. Max cannot reach out to—let alone get involved with—mirror images.

There are other destructive aspects of the popularity contest. Consider how it leads to hopelessness. Since it is not possible to please everyone and certainly not possible to be admired by everyone, complete popular success is impossible to achieve. Even partial success is difficult to attain. Worse yet, whatever popular success is achieved doesn't help an iota to make it with Max. On the contrary, the result to Max is detrimental. Thus, the general effect is one of hopelessness and is depressing indeed. The attempt to please everyone creates a multifaceted mirror reflecting what one *thinks* other people desire. Making oneself a mirror destroys the feeling for one's own identity, crippling self-esteem and ultimately destroying happiness and success.

Now, you may ask, "What does this all have to do with me? All I want is to make it with the people who are important to me." If this is so, fine! But you would be amazed at how many people lose sight of the real goal and with little or no awareness at all become sucked into the popularity morass. So, please, please, remember—our goal is not popularity. You are important and Max is important and our all-important concern is with what happens between you and Max.

What does Max see?

Looks are an asset and those who have them are fortunate. However, very few of us are blessed with perfect features and even more fortunately, very few of us really need them. This is so because Max sees much more than he sees. What does he see? Max really sees what he feels and you, too, see what you feel. Another way of saying this is that what Max feels very much affects what he sees. As a matter of fact, what Max feels has much more of an effect on what he sees than what he sees does on what he feels. This is not a play on words. Actually, this is so important that we must be careful not to oversimplify. Max's feelings are all-important because they are so intimately linked with his impressions of you. This includes his initial impressions as well as the ever-changing impressions he will have throughout his relationship with you. Now, these impressions are based on Max and his personal history and what he brings to his encounter with you and what is there in him long before the two of you make contact. Max brings his concept of himself, which he will amply demonstrate to you if you just see, hear, feel. He brings his feelings and values and also his distortions and prejudices regarding people. He brings a history of the experiences he has had with men and women and especially with the first man and woman in his life—his father and mother. In short, he brings the effects of the highly complex experiences of having been a person for a number of years. Now, he will respond to *you* and it is your turn to add your impact to his store-house of human experiences. Let me say that his impressions of you and yours of him begin much earlier than you

215

may think. They start with the very first time you've heard of each other, telephoned or even glanced in one another's direction. Human relationships start much earlier than people suspect and however subtle these beginnings may be, they are very important. You would be amazed at how much Max and you, too, pick up at a glance. I use the word "glance" here most broadly, so as to include sound, smell, sight and everything in himself that Max feels with. We cannot do much about Max's history. But what about you? How about you yourself and your effect on Max? Of course, you will have an individual effect, uniquely your own, since you, too, were there long before you met Max. This effect is all-important because later on you can examine it and you can determine what you can do about it, but—and this is a big but—Max's impression of you, how he feels about you, how he sees you, will largely depend on how you feel about you and how you see yourself!

How you feel about you shows

How you see yourself, that is, how you feel about you is all-important for so many reasons. Obviously, your feelings about you affects you in every phase of your life. But for us, here, an all-important aspect of how you feel about you is *that it shows.* As your relationship with Max goes on in time beyond the first second and even during the first "glance," how *you* feel about you will play an infinitely greater role than your superficial features. To me, it is not amazing at all that so many people who got *to know* Eleanor Roosevelt felt that she became more and more beautiful as they continued to *see* her. I am convinced that this in large part was due to her own feelings of growth, as well as her growing self-acceptance.

Yes, how you feel about you shows. How? In everything, absolutely everything you do or, for that matter, avoid doing. Max is not dull. He may not feel all of it and he may not verbalize any of it. But he feels enough to have multiple accurate impressions of how you feel about you and these will certainly affect him. I use the word *"feel"* because *"feel"* is exactly what I mean and because the *feeling* Max has encompasses the totality of how he experiences you with all of his senses. So, how do you show it? Inadvertently in many ways and I hope this doesn't make you self-conscious. Our goal is definitely not to cover up your feelings about you. Besides which, you simply can't. Our goal is making it with Max on a healthy, sustained, give-and-take basis. Even if it were possible, subterfuge would sabotage our goal, as it invariably impairs one's relating ability. You show how you feel about you in the way you walk, gesture, talk, question, respond, things you talk about, things you avoid talking about, your interests, lack of interests, the ways you embrace, kiss, shake hands, write, sing, laugh, cry and emote and don't emote, drink, dress, furnish your apartment, in the hobbies you choose, the work you do and your attitude toward it, the things you laugh at and get angry at, and the list goes on and on. The point is that your every expression and every action is an expression of you and gives important information about you, about your patterns of behavior, that is, how you conduct your life vis-à-vis people and how you feel about you. Max does not sit down and analyze all this. He does not consciously add, subtract and divide. But unconscious automatic calculations are always taking place, and they create impressions. These impressions are very greatly affected by the most

217

important impression of all—namely, the impression that you have of you, yourself. This impression invariably gets through to him and will most strongly affect how he feels about you and the relationship you are both participating in.

There's no place like home

Of course, how Max feels about Max will get through to you. The interaction between Max and you, and you and Max, is a very complicated one. But there is little you can do about past history, either his or yours. Also, unless your relationship becomes sustained and very special, there is little you can do about Max's impression of himself. That leaves you. In order to generate really constructive stuff *now* we must look to you. The only one we can do something about at this point is *you* and *you* are the only one to do it. *But*—and this is a most important *but*—you must be *you* and nobody else.

There is no place like home because home is yourself and there is no better person to be than *you*. Again, this is so for so many reasons. The energy expended to be someone other than yourself is an enormous waste, since you cannot possibly succeed in shedding your own skin, besides which—chances are you would never make the exchange, even if it were possible, once you really got to know yourself and the fellow you would change with. However, it is in terms of Max that being yourself really pays off. Any *act* to be other than you, any affectation on your part, if not immediately, then eventually, will be perceived by Max. He may be too polite to say anything or he may be too compassionate to hurt you, or he may not have even verbalized your *phoniness* to himself. He may not be conscious of it. But make no mistake—in his guts, where he lives and where he is motivated to decision and action, he will know that he is not dealing with the real you and he will resent it and will very likely reject you. He may also interpret "acting" or "exaggeration" or "affectation" on your part as a certain sign of inadequacy and even dishonesty, which may well repel him.

On rare occasions, an "act" may seem to work. But if this happens, it is not a good sign. The individual who responds to an act is usually a "play actor" himself, and is not Max at all. It is a sad business, indeed, when two actors remove their masks and find that they actually have nothing whatsoever in common to sustain a real relationship. A relationship between masks is just that and must not be confused with the real stuff that goes on between two real people. If Max is initially and momentarily attracted by "an act," you can be sure that no act, however ingeniously played, will intrigue him for an extended period of time. Again and again, I have seen "adults" (especially in vacation resorts among strangers) bantering up and back, often with great underlying hostility, in an obvious act intended to impress each other with smart talk and seeming sophistication. Be sure that Max, whoever he is, will take no part in this kind of adolescent loser enterprise.

For a worthwhile constructive relationship to take place, we must first have two people, two real people. For this, there is absolutely no substitute. So we must deal with you, the *real you*, whatever you are. Of course, you as a person are a combination of many factors; as already discussed, we all have our assets and limitations.

Being and becoming and yesterday, today and later

At this point, I want to talk about a few concepts that have a philosophical ring, but which will also have an important practical purpose in making it with ourselves and Max.

The present, the living present, is all-important because in fact that is all there is. Yesterday is gone. Tomorrow is not yet here. There is only *now*, and what you are *now* and not what you used to be or desire to become. The only living and relating that we do is in the present —*now*.

Being is a short term I want to use to represent *living* as you are, *accepting* who you are, in this moment and in each moment that is the *present—now*.

Becoming, on the other hand, connotes self-glorification, compulsive striving, superficial attempts at a shot in the arm, and in short, becoming that which you are not, in other words, self-rejection.

Being is infinitely more rewarding than becoming. This is so because if we are really involved in whatever it is we are being, we are really involved in *now*, in relating to ourselves and in relating to Max. The preoccupation with becoming something is invariably linked to future dreams of glory and dissipates much energy in useless anticipation. Similarly, the waste, if anything, is even greater, complaining or dreaming of a past that cannot be changed, undone or recaptured. There is only this moment and a fuller involvement in the process of being whatever it is we are in this moment fulfills the future. This is so for two reasons. First, our relatively total involvement in *now* contributes to better development and

220

growth so that we will be better candidates for a future *now*. Secondly, having developed the habit of living *now*, of *being*, when the future has arrived and becomes the present, it, too, will get the complete attention, involvement and respect that only *now* deserves. Thus, we may say that a healthy cycle has been established. I am not suggesting that one should not plan for the future or have plans for a better future, etc. But, I am saying that anticipation can snowball into more anticipation and a wasteful involvement with a day and a role and a person that never quite arrives. For example, the premedical student immersed in the future glories of the great medical practitioner he will become lacks involvement in the premedical work of now. This sabotage of his relationship with Max (here his teachers and his work) will seriously hinder his future medical work and may even destroy the possibility of future *nows* as a medical student and practitioner.

What does all this have to do with Max? Everything! Because Max and you must relate *now* if the relating that goes on between you is to reach a more and more effective state of being. Your relationship is not a static entity. Of course, it will not just be there suddenly and completely in full bloom. It is an ever-developing and ever-changing process and hopefully will be evergrowing in a constructive and fruitful direction. This can only happen if you go on to know yourself and each the other, more and more, in as open a way as possible. Open to what? Open to each other without prejudice, without prejudgment and with a willingness to learn. Above all, you must be open to allow involvement in whatever is between you to take place *now*, with you *being* you. All this is not easy, especially in the beginning. Most of us are, to a considerable extent, involved in *becoming*. But things will get easier and with work and patience, a greater state of *being* and making it with Max will evolve.

This is the enemy

This is the enemy—you carry him around with you wherever you go. He robs you of energy, time and freedom. He destroys your potential for happiness and success. He stands as a barrier between you and yourself and you and other people.

What can you do?

Get to know him in his various roles as best you can. Get to recognize his many manifestations. *Become conscious and aware* of the ways in which you are self-sabotaging, hurting and defeating. Consciousness, awareness and hard work can help you to extricate yourself from the "loser" morass.

I spoke earlier of self-delusion, affectation, pretense and what generally comes through as phoniness and a lack of self-esteem. Unfortunately, there are still other enemies we must be wary of. Indeed, these may well be your worst enemies. I speak here of self-hate, hopelessness, cynicism, bitterness and routine complaining. These very serious detriments to your well-being and to making it with Max can be expressed blatantly and overtly or may be very subtle in their expression. There are many people who feel enormous contempt for themselves and express this contempt habitually and constantly and with an almost total lack of awareness. Statements like:

"I am not really much."

"I am really not that good at anything."

"Me? What do I know?"

"Who am I to have an opinion?"

"Nothing good ever happens to me."

"This is a rotten world and I know it."

"What's the use of trying?"

"Nothing really changes."

"One of these days, the big blast will knock us off, anyway."

"I don't believe in doctors—either you get well on your own or you die."

"Psychiatry can't help anyone."

"People are all lousy."

"A girl doesn't stand a chance."

"Over 30? Forget it!"

"Nothing but kooks around—all girls, kooks."

"Men—let's not talk about them."

often demonstrate a way of life and an extremely destructive outlook. The people making these statements are often unaware that they are expressing self-hate, cynicism, hopelessness and bitterness. There are more subtle ways, of course—dressing in an increasingly dowdy way; taking fewer and fewer vacations; eating poorer and poorer lunches, attending fewer and fewer social events, getting fat and still fatter, expressing self-doubt in false grandiosity and false modesty, a general inability to engage in pleasurable activity, a predilection for damaging and generally unrewarding relationships, taking jobs inappropriate to one's ability and sustaining them despite boredom and poor remuneration, a great capacity to get involved in situations that produce suffering, accident proneness, losing objects, an inability to accept gifts graciously and enjoyably, and an inability to accept compliments, an inability to take one's self, opinions and feelings with either humor or seriousness, constantly derogating one's obvious assets, having an ugly mind's eye picture of oneself, seeing everybody else as better looking and brainier than oneself, going into situations

223

(exams, interviews, jobs, etc.) unprepared, getting sick or tired just before an enjoyable possibility is in the offing, a predilection for disastrous financial involvements, an inability to spend money on oneself, etc., etc., etc.

Self-hate is a particularly bad one. Believe it or not, the enemy uses this form in an attempt to convince you that you are trying to help yourself. It goes something like this—"If I hate myself enough, I'll spur myself on to bigger and better things." "If I am enough of a martyr, through beating myself enough, the world will take pity and somehow good things will come my way." It is sad indeed to see a patient in consultation who, without awareness, is in effect saying the following—"Can't understand it. I've been full of self-hate all these years; I treated myself very badly; God knows how I've suffered. When does my turn come—I mean, when does something good happen to me?" The answer is—it doesn't! That is, unless you make it happen, and self-hate will certainly block the way. Be it subtle or blatant, short-lived or chronic, the effects are always the same. It leads to inhibitions and paralysis, loss of time, loss of energy, stagnation and a breakdown in successful relating. If strong enough, it can lead to severe depression and even suicide.

Hopelessness can justifiably be called malignant

It permeates everything one does or doesn't do. It disastrously affects every aspect of one's life. It pollutes the environment so that in a contagious way, it depresses everybody in contact with its particular victim.

Its effect is inhibiting, stultifying and even paralyzing. It links to self-hate, and each complements the other in producing a walking dead man, whose only sign of life is an occasional *self-beating*. Hopelessness is the great enemy of spontaneity and aliveness. It is the principal energy used to convert a live man into a mechanical man. No other form of the enemy is more anti-health and pro-sickness. It is the great guard of neurosis. The individual who feels hopeless is convinced that people don't change and can't change. He is convinced that people can't resolve conflicts or take responsibility for their lives. He is convinced that we are only helpless will-o'-the-wisps. He feels that nothing he does will change things, anyway— so why do it? In this way, he very capably and effectively protects his neurotic status quo, hopelessness serving as an impenetrable armor.

Much hopelessness comes from inordinate demands on ourselves. Those of us who expect to be ever-loving and ever-loved, ever admired and complete masters of all situations, free of all conflicts and burdensome involvement, perfect lovers, perfect friends, brilliant adversaries, etc., etc., etc., will of course suffer from repeated severe disappointments. These disappointments coupled with the increasing (and hidden) realization that these exorbitant unrealistic goals can never be fulfilled lead to hopelessness. To the extent that these neurotic goals can be surrendered, to the extent that the individual can replace fantastic demands with realistic aspirations and values based on real human assets and limitations, to the extent that he can come down to earth from godlike self-illusions, he will mitigate, neutralize and even obliterate hopelessness.

Of course, hopelessness also exists both subtly and severely. We all feel hopelessness at times in a small way. There are all degrees. But whatever the degree, and however subtle the manifestations, this form of the enemy is always destructive. Well, don't fall for hopelessness, however it's presented! People can and do change. People grow and they get healthier. To the extent that they can give up ridiculous aspirations, they can tap real resources and achieve real self-fulfillment. Sometimes they need help to do this—but competent help works (See Section V). Believe it! Don't sink into the hopelessness morass! If you feel yourself slipping, have a talk with yourself. Have you been too demanding of yourself and of life? What can you do? Is getting more hopeless and self-hating going to bring you any real reward? Of course not! So, get out there and pitch if you can! If you can't, then get somebody to help you do just that!

Guilt, envy and jealousy are other common forms of the enemy. I call these the great evaders. What are you evading? Living! How can you relate to Max on a successful level when you substitute guilt for responsibility? How can you have sufficient energy and time for relating which is the stuff of real living when you occupy yourself with envy and jealousy? These are corrosive and destructive forces because they create emotional isolation from other people. They result in sitting in one's own juice and stewing. They are really self-digestive processes, which ultimately contribute to self-hate, hate for everyone else and emotional isolation from everyone else. This isolation results in a further self-hating process and in increasing hopelessness about relating to other people, thus promoting a very destructive vicious cycle. Jealousy and envy, as well as guilt, simply remove you from other people and any possible success with them. They hurt relationships with people, do not contribute to world improvement, and seldom hurt their objects. The ultimate destructive aspects of envy or jealousy, experienced as lack of energy, time and success, as well as· increased cynicism, bitterness and loss of enjoyable living, are confined to the individual who suffers attack by these enemies.

Now, what about Max in all this? Let me say that you have been living with yourself for years. You are the expert and Max will take your evaluation of you very seriously. Max is relatively healthy. He is not a masochist or a sadist, nor is he a lifesaver. He will not devote his precious time in a heroic effort to convince you that you are not a psychic cripple. Moreover, he will certainly not join you in a *let's beat you up session*. If you, in effect, say that you are hopeless, then he will probably believe that you are in fact hopeless. If you will reject you, then he will reject you. Martyrdom, if anything, will repel him, as will complaining, self-abusive and constant expressions of abuse by an uncaring world. There is little that is as boring and torturous as attempting to relate to an individual who is totally preoccupied with injustice-collecting. In the very beginning of relating to you, Max as yet has made very little emotional investment in you. Since he is an emotionally serious person, he will be careful of where he makes these most important investments. So, as yet, there is nothing to hold him, and Max will run and will run fast in search of a person who believes in herself and who shows it in expressions of real self-esteem. This kind of person is *alive* and knows it and lets Max know it. She does not project the feeling to Max that a relationship with her will give him the opportunity of walking among cemetery stones. This person is coping well with the aforementioned enemies. Her emotional economy is a good one. But more about that in Section V.

The self story

I spoke earlier of self and being onself and needing a self to relate to Max with. Well, let's go into the self story a little more.

Another way of referring to self is by use of the word "identity," that is, *who* you are. It is all-important to have a feeling for who you are because it is your identity, yourself, which is the single, most powerful instrument you will ever have with which to relate to Max.

Who are you or what are you? You have a body. You have assets. You have goals and aspirations and an intellect and feelings about people and events and things. You have desires and appetites and frustrations and potential in various areas and problems and limitations, too. All these comprise your identity, your *self*, and the more realistic your concept of you is, the more self you will have to relate to Max with.

However, I want to speak of an area of self, knowledge of which will be even more important in relating to Max. Indeed, this aspect of self is the very stuff of identity and may be considered the very anatomical cornerstone of self. I speak here of *values*. Values are the basis of our emotional and social lives. They will determine what we are and where we are going and what we do with our energy, time and assets and how, and with what, and with whom, we get involved. They will describe what is important to us, relatively important, very important and not important at all. For example: To some of us, family, friends, work are very important. To some, honesty, honor, country, community, relatedness are very important. To some, scholarly veracity is most important.

To some, money, power and prestige are very important. To others, God and religion are most important. Of course, each of us will have our own particular combination of values and our own individual identities with which we relate to Max. There are many of us, however, whose values are very shaky and even nonexistent. Here, we often see people who are responding to compulsions, rather than values, and often to compulsions of which they are not aware. Since some of these compulsions or compelling needs are in conflict with each other, it is small wonder that these people feel torn apart, fragmented and sometimes indecisive to the point of paralysis.

Now it is most important to be able to differentiate a value from a compulsion and wherever possible to replace compulsions with values. I describe the difference in Section II under "Muddles." However, this area is so important that I want to go into it in greater detail in the next chapter.

Values, choice, compulsions and freedom

How can we tell the difference and how do we arrive at values? There is a vast difference between:

1) I feel like doing and I decide and I do or I don't do, and

2) I must do or not do or it's the thing to do or everybody does and I do accordingly.

In (1) my feelings are very much in evidence and I consult myself, and how and what I feel. If necessary, I allow myself to be in conflict and to struggle through my conflict to a decision. The decision I arrive at is uniquely my own and born of my freedom to struggle through my feelings to either act or not act. Do not confuse struggling with lack of freedom. On the contrary, it takes personal health and freedom to participate in one's own feelings and to struggle in order to make a free choice. Here in (1) doing or not doing, action or nonaction, is a flexible matter, so that a change of mind is always a possibility. In this kind of free choosing, one acts in his own behalf and not in a rigid, unbreakable, contractual agreement with oneself. This kind of freedom to feel and to decide and if necessary, to experience conflict and to struggle through conflict to an answer, produces values. This kind of tapping one's own feelings and arriving at one's own individual values produces a sense of self-responsibility and identity. This produces a *self* with which to relate to Max, plus the ways and hows one relates vis-à-vis Max.

(2) is born of an automatic choiceless adherence to rules learned and ingested long ago of which the individual may be unaware. These rules are tyrannical, uncompromising taskmasters. Obedience is rigidly black or white, choiceless, and allows no deviation whatsoever. While knowledge of the rule may be absent (unconscious), reaction to it is obvious in the rigid pattern of behavior the individual is cramped into. Obedience is strict, total and any attempt to veer from what feels like a contractual agreement produces anxiety, guilt and self-punishment, often in the form of depression and even suicide. In (2), immediate automatic adherence to "the rules" blocks the individual from struggle, from decision and from the production of values, and from further responsibility for self and from growth. What one really feels plays almost no role and the individual—a loser—goes through life feeling that he has not been at all consulted in actions concerning himself, and indeed he

hasn't. He feels that he is a will-o'-the wisp, blown this way and that; he often projects his anger at enslavement and lack of self-respect to Max. He irrationally comes to feel that Max and other people have always pushed him around. This is largely so because, lacking a healthy respect for his own feelings and opinions, he is always unduly concerned with what other people think. A casual remark is often interpreted as a harsh criticism or a command. Of course, this kind of response to inner tyranny and its destructive effects on relating to other people, stunts personal growth and hampers the development of a stronger feeling for self through struggle. People in this position are often very sensitive to coercion. They must either slavishly comply with the mildest suggestion or throw it out completely. They cannot weigh the pros and cons to decide whether or not the suggestion has merit in their own particular framework of feelings.

I remember a patient, Mary, who hated to go out with more than one girl friend at a time. She said she had no trouble when she was out with only one friend. After several sessions, her difficulties began to make sense. Mary was a compulsively compliant person and formed relationships with friends who seemed like leaders—decision-makers. Her two best friends were Betty and Jo Anne. When she went out with either, everything was fine. Betty or Jo Anne directed, Mary complied and felt "liked" and comfortable. But when she went out with both her friends, she occasionally ran into very uncomfortable situations. Both Betty and Jo Anne were "headstrong." Mary described one occasion. "Betty wanted to go to the Capitol, but Jo Anne decided to go to Radio City Music Hall. They couldn't agree and decided to go their separate ways. I felt torn apart. They are both great girls and I didn't want to disappoint either one of them. I wanted them both to like me. Yet, how could I please both of them at the same

231

time? I got a terrible headache and went home. You know something—I had that headache for days. I hope they didn't feel offended."

Of course, Mary was in conflict and chose to develop a headache rather than to struggle through to a solution. But the real pity is that she saw the solution only in terms of pleasing Betty or Jo Anne. It never occurred to her that pleasing herself was a possible solution. She did not consult herself or her own feelings. She did not allow herself to have any feeling about which film she would prefer. Her concern was with her friends and her compulsion to be liked. She completely neglected an all-important person in her life—herself. An avoidance of struggle in this way certainly detracts from the development of self.

I couldn't help thinking of Betty and Jo Anne and their relationship with Mary. Were they relieved to see her go home? Do they see her as a drag, a nonentity or a willing kind of space-occupying fixture, a pawn? In any case, this is certainly not a maximum Max relationship.

101 maximum Max questions

Asking and answering these questions is an exercise designed to "open doors" to possibilities of making it with Max.

All the questions are directly related to "winning" through "Maximum Max" relating. Ask them of yourself slowly and carefully. Mull them over several times.

1. *Are you aware that we all share a common sea of air?* Two people—any two people—however different, have more in common than they have apart. Yes, the

"arch criminal" and the "most saintly benefactor of mankind" both belong to the same species and both breathe the same air. Surely, the potential for communicating and relating must be there among us—if we want it.

2. *Do you make statements like, "Maybe I'm too old to change" or "But, I never did it before"?* You may be caught in *status quo quicksand.* This may be linked to the *"If it isn't familiar, leave me out"* syndrome (see Familiar and Unfamiliar Muddle, Section II). Are you aware of how destructive this attitude is to the possibility of newer and healthier ways of relating? Are you aware of how this curtails the possibility of new and possibly rewarding relationships?

3. *Do you make statements like, "I don't care," "Couldn't interest me less," "Can't be bothered," "I mind my own business—strictly!"?* Remember that you cannot relate successfully on a noninvolvement basis. You may succeed in feeling that you have risen above people, issues and activities, but you may also find yourself stranded, alone and bored, let alone a failure in relating to Max, whoever he is.

4. *Do you know that loneliness, emptiness, and the fear of death are often self-generated?* They are often related to deadening one's own feelings and to lack of investment of feelings in other people.

5. *Are you waiting to be "motivated" or for an "urge" to hit you before you become "involved"?* This is often putting the cart before the horse. We must "try" something before we know enough about it to feel motivated to further "trying." It takes an act of willpower to break up inertia so as to promote initial involvement. After we feel involvement, motivation can take place which will lead to fuller involvement. If you do nothing and wait for an "urge" to get involved with people, you may, at the end

233

of a lifetime, find that the only thing you have been involved in is—waiting.

6. *Do you know the difference between resignation and acceptance?* In a given situation (or concerning a given relationship) in *resignation,* you compulsively feel that you cannot do anything to change it. You are virtually paralyzed. In *acceptance,* you have a choice—you can change it if you want to, but you *choose* to keep its status quo.

7. *Have you considered that if you "don't make waves," nobody including yourself will know that you are alive?*

8. *Are you caught in the love trap?* This is the "everybody has to like me" morass. This is the "peace at any cost" swamp. The *cost* is usually a steady chronic erosion of your *self* until Max feels that he is relating to nobody at all. Are you aware that no matter how you "act," *everybody* will not like you? Are you aware that no matter how you try to "please," some people will continue to like you while others don't? Are you aware that whether you are liked or not by "most" people, will have no practical effect on your life whatsoever? Are you aware that you must like you in order to be a winner? Are you aware that every compulsive effort to "be liked" will be rewarded with self-hate, hidden rage, injustice-collecting and feelings of martyrdom? Are you aware of how destructive these are in relating to Max? Do you predicate your life on *"what people will think"?* Are you aware that they are mostly concerned with their own lives and deep relationships, and their own problems? Do you have trouble saying no? Do you know that this makes for duplicitous role-playing? This robs you of the opportunity for real relationships! Have you taken a chance lately? I mean in any situation, a chance on catering to yourself rather than the need to be liked. Do you know that after you try once

you will find it easier to try again? This process can even contribute to you liking you and to real maximum relating to Max.

9. *Are you aware that many relationships are not Max relationships at all?* Are you aware that many relationships are, in fact, destructive enterprises? They rob you of time, energy and self—all of which can be used for Max relating. Have you reevaluated lately? How about the people with whom you have a "losing" enterprise going? What has kept you there? Are you caught in the status quo morass? Familiarity? Are you bogged down by the "nice guy" role? Are you sucked in by the "I understand his problem" dodge? You can understand someone's problem and still not want to be martyred by it. Are you aware that taking a chance and breaking a loser relationship is as constructive as taking a chance and getting involved in a Max relationship? When you extricate yourself from a poisonous encounter, are you aware that you are treating both you and the other guy with real dignity and respect?

10. *Are you aware that anger is a perfectly normal human emotion?* Are you aware that many of us often pervert this emotion extraordinarily—always to our own detriment? Are you aware that repressed anger snowballs and is often converted to anxiety? Are you aware that when we repress anger, we often also repress love? Are you aware that anger can be a warm, communicative, human emotion, but when repressed, can become cold, lingering, vindictive and corrosive? Are you aware that anger in itself will not hurt let alone kill anybody? Getting angry and getting it out—expressing it, clears the air and permits communication to take place. Are you aware that a temper tantrum is not the equivalent of going crazy, that it may, in fact, put you in a position of relief and greater rationality? Are you aware that children often

need and ask for an angry response from you so that they can feel its warmth, your interest and the limits within which they must behave?

11. *Are you a contestant in the Big Race?* This is a real self-grinder! This is part of and feeds the popularity contest. This makes for competition with everybody, a need for praise and admiration from everybody and a need for mastery of every situation. It leaves no time or energy for self or for real relating. Are you aware that there are people who predicate their lives on vengeance and on a vindictive triumph? Nothing is more corrosive, empty and finally lacking in satisfaction. Do you fear helplessness? Are you aware that to be helpless is not to be hopeless? Helplessness at times is an inherent part of the human condition. If you succeed in putting everyone down—if you win in this area—do you know that you lose? Do you know that there are people who cannot tolerate praise of anyone else? For them, there is only one beauty, one intellect, one talent.

12. *Are you aware that the need for perfection can lead to hopelessness and paralysis?* A need to relate to only perfect people can result in total solitude. Are you one of those people who needs 100 percent to pass? If so, the strain on you and Max is intolerable.

13. *Do you know anyone who feels that they ought to know everything without learning?* These are people who always say, "I know, I know," before any explanation even gets under way. "Born knowing" as I call this affliction, destroys the possibility of openness, learning and real knowing.

14. *Can you "let go" and "live and let live" or must you effect super control of yourself and everyone else?*

15. *How much do you do for pride and how much do you do for yourself and Max?* Pride is on one wavelength. You and Max are on quite another.

16. *Are you aware that prejudice and prejudgment ("I know him, them, that kind") aside from other corrosive effects precludes the enriching experience of many potential Max relationships?*

17. *Where is the focus?* Is it always out there? Is it always the other guy who is responsible? Who is doing your living, the other guy or you?

18. *Are you a victim of the big paradox?* Simply stated, you are not getting nearly as much out of life as it has to offer; yet, you want much more than life has to offer. Are you aware that people and people relationships have limitations? Are you aware that the human condition—life on Earth—has inherent limitations? Are you aware that only involvement in the everyday bread-and-butter here and now is for real and contains real success in terms of happiness?

19. *Do you have a forgotten child, namely the child in you?* Have you forgotten your own youth and childhood and its limitations, tribulations, jolts, struggles and trials and errors? Refreshing your memory will help to make it with Max, especially when Max is a child or a young adult.

Remember that every generation has its adolescent language, way of dress, etc. This is a natural and normal way of exploring and developing the solidification of self necessary for adulthood. If you are not closed and judgmental, but keep the lines of communication open, Max will return when he has satisfied his useful need to explore, at which time he will have much more in common with you on an adult level. Do you know that young people are especially zealous about their privacy and ownership? This is a natural part of developing a sense of self and individuality. Do not breach this need for privacy! Remember how you were affected by dogmatism and being patronized, so teach but don't preach!

20. *Have you considered that perfection exists only in death?* Death is total and complete.

21. *Do you feel that there is nearly always a choice?* Good! Because in relating, in relating situations, there are almost always a number of good choices. Danger usually lies more in inertia than in making a bad choice.

22. *In making a decision, do you use your whole self?* Is it a visceral thing—springing from the guts—or do you arrive at a conclusion through pure logic without tuning in to how you feel? Or is it an integration of both?

23. *Can you accept a mistake without committing yourself to an onslaught of self-hate?* Do you look back on mistakes and carry a grudge against yourself ad infinitum? If you do, are you aware that you probably exert the same intolerable pressure on Max?

24. *Are you aware that your most important decision involves the choice you make as to whom you choose to relate to deeply?*

25. *In making a decision, if you get anxious, do you pay attention to that anxiety?* If you don't, you may lose an opportunity for self-exploration. The anxiety may be a clue that in your guts you are at odds with a particular decision.

26. *Do you know that however close two people are, they still remain two individuals?* Individuals do need occasional privacy, which is in no way evidence of lack of love.

27. *Are you aware that taking an individual for granted is extremely destructive to Max relationships?*

28. *If you want a raise, do you ask for it?* How else will your boss know?

29. *In a partnership, which is more important—* winning an argument? Affixing the blame? Or sharing the responsibility and clarifying issues?

30. *If you and Max are caught in an attack of sus-*

tained sullen silent anger, will you break the pride dead-lock or wait and wait and wait?

31. *Are you aware that even the most loving parents deserve to be alone and away from their children at times?* The kids deserve this break, too.

32. *When you have to make a speech, are you terrified?* Have you considered that you are not a performer, that you are not there for admiration and that you don't have to "do something" for which you are not equipped? You are probably there to give information, which you are well equipped to do. If you do not demand the impossible of yourself—that is, a stellar performance—chances are you will cut your anxiety by 98 percent and make it with Max as an audience.

33. *When you are at a "no exit party," do you leave or stay for the mutual torture?* I call a room full of totally incompatible people a "no exit party."

34. *Do you waste the precious and limited time of your life impossibly trying to make up for disappointing past events?*

35. *Do you spend most of your relating time in mutual caring and sharing?* Are you aware of how few people can resist real caring or a demonstration of *real* interest in them?

36. *Do you construct problems in order to feel alive?* Are you aware that peace is peace and not deadness and that life is life and not turmoil and chaos?

37. *Are you aware that your boss will be most impressed with real involvement in your work?*

38. *Are you aware that many disagreements are due to the fact that the words mean different things to the antagonists?* People who stop and ask "What is he really saying" may find that they don't disagree at all. They can then "talk."

39. *Are you aware of the power of an apology?* It can advance a communicating experience mightily.

40. *Are you involved in the Big Exchange—emotional sharing and caring and involving?*

41. *Do you know that "mine and yours" bank accounts are often linked to separate emotional, as well as money, accounts?*

42. *Do you know that no amount of money helps a man to cheat death?* Have you considered that money can represent work and emotional involvement and as such, is a communicating and sharing substance among people?

43. *Do you know that one antidote for self-consciousness is increased real interest in other people?*

44. *Do you know that questions like "How do you feel?" and statements like "Take care of yourself" can be bridges between two people when they spring from real concern?*

45. *Can you accept presents without having to quickly reciprocate so as not be beholden?* If you can't, chances are that you are afraid to be involved.

46. *Have you experienced the exciting tremendous results of being open and nonjudgmental in a state of exchanging all emotions including warm anger and warm love?*

47. *Have you experienced the "glow" that follows a real compliment?*

48. *Do you tend to argue or to look for where the breakdown in communication has taken place?*

49. *Do you agree with me that relationships do not remain static?* They either grow or die.

50. *Do you put yourself on the line and reap the rewards of responsibility?* Do you tell people how you really feel—not to hurt—but to truly represent your *self*? Do you take a chance on not being liked—at least now and then?

51. *Do you take a chance with the "unfamiliar" and*

*with "doing" which leads to self-esteem and more doing
and creates a healthy cycle?*

52. *When you want to know, do you ask?*

53. *Do you play a role or yourself?*

54. *When you have an urge to "run away," have you
considered "running into" instead?*

55. *Do you realize that "feeling" involves pain as
well as pleasure, but anesthesia is deathlike?*

56. *Are you dedicated to stagnation or to possible
change?*

57. *Are you aware that fear of failure can prevent
participation and success?* It can hide enormous vanity
and need for perfection.

58. *Do you know that the ability to allow one's self
to encounter "real problems" (not drummed up, imagined
ones) can result in growth?* If you want "it"—anything—
to happen, you can't sit on the side and wait for "it" to
happen. You have to make "it" happen. This applies tenfold in making it with Max.

59. *Is struggling worth it?* It certainly isn't if it is
done for the sake of suffering. If struggling takes place
for the sake of self and values, it can be rewarding indeed. Of course, this is not easy. It often involves sitting
with discomfort for awhile rather than jumping out of it.
This requires patience and putting off immediate satisfaction. With practice, however, one's frustration tolerance can grow.

60. *Do you remember that anxiety can lead to confusion, but that confusion can lead to greater clarity?*

61. *Do you remember that you can't please everybody, you can't master every situation and you can't
"rise above" all situations and still be working in the
service of you and Max?* When did you last take a chance
on not being liked; not being the boss; and on not run-

241

ning away from a "mishmash" with other people? This may make you anxious, but what a payoff!

62. *"How do I help myself to take a constructive chance"?* I try not to miss an opportunity to feel and to desire even if it means a struggle and anxiety and confusion. A feeling may not be pleasant. It may not fit in with the easiest or most compatible pattern of the moment, but I don't throw it away. It is too valuable. I don't get frightened! A feeling is not an action. Do you know that the more you allow yourself to feel, the more real freedom of action you will have?

"I feel!" "I like!" "I don't like!" "I want!" To have a real strong feeling—how wonderful! To have a real choice about what you want to do and to do it and to take responsibility for doing it, this is the stuff of *self,* necessary to making it with Max.

63. *Will you cheat yourself from getting professional help should you feel you need it?*

64. *When have you "cared" about somebody else even more than for yourself in a healthy way?* This means not to the exclusion of yourself, but rather concomitant with caring about yourself.

65. *Do you allow yourself reevaluations as to job, study, friends, etc.?* Reevaluation means just that and may or may not lead to action. It does, however, point to self-confidence and a willingness to struggle through conflicting feelings if necessary for personal growth.

66. *Can you take action because you feel like it and because you like yourself or must you generate anger and even rage to give you the push?*

67. *Have you considered that getting involved with anybody or anything does not necessarily mean a permanent contract?* People can, if they only will, permit themselves to step out of, as well as into, relationships.

68. *Do you feel that time is NOW or are you waiting*

*and waiting to praise, to care, to express warmth, to share
and to begin to live?*

69. *Have you thought that if you change you, you
change the world?* You are part of this world. If you become healthier, your children and Max, whoever he is,
must profit from contact with you.

70. *Do you spend a major part of your "happy times"
in the past while the here and now drifts away?*

71. *Are you a "yes man," a "multifaceted mirror," or
do you let people know what you really feel?*

72. *How much energy and time do you use in pleasing others and how much in your own behalf?*

73. *Are you aware of the power of the statement, "I
was wrong" in improving communications?*

74. *Are you aware that "gratuitous information" is
seldom appreciated?* Professional analysts only analyze in
their offices and get paid.

75. *Are you aware that compulsive conformity is just
as sick as compulsive rebellion?*

76. *Have you been striving to be "average," "normal"
and "dead" in the feeling department?*

77. *Is there any "lazy" person who is not resigned or
hopeless or chronically depressed or in some way does not
suffer from physiological or psychological difficulty?*

78. *Have you found out that the compulsively self-
effacing person often has more real inner strength than
the compulsively aggressive person?*

79. *Do you pay as much attention to what you feel
as you do to what you think?*

80. *Are you waiting for the world to change? What
are you doing to change yourself?*

81. *Can you allow yourself to be frustrated and to
stay frustrated for awhile in order to find real clarification?*

82. *Are you aware that some people are closer during "arguments" than when they are "at peace"?*

83. *When someone says (or yells) something derogatory, do you assume that they have you in mind?*

84. *Do you know that "glibness" and being exceedingly "articulate" are not synonymous with brilliance or profundity?* But do you know that "still waters" often don't run very deep?

85. *Are you aware that weeping, screaming, a warm bath or taking a long walk can bring great relief?* None are signs of weakness.

86. *Have you been fading out?* Do you feel that you don't count in things? How much effort have you expended in counting and in getting involved?

87. *Do you get into arguments (particularly ones involving semantics) where due to deft logic, you win, while in your guts you know that there is something you have lost?* You may have lost an opportunity to really communicate honestly on a feeling level.

88. *Are you aware that "struggling" and "openness" and "involvement" with people bring more wisdom than old age does?*

89. *Are you more concerned with what should be or with what is?*

90. *Are you "listening" to Max when he talks or are you "waiting" for him to finish?*

91. *Do you, again and again, seek a "good mama" or a "good papa" who will in some magical way make up for all past hurts—OR—do you look for adult Max relationships?*

92. *Are you waiting to be "discovered"?*

93. *Are you bored?* Have you had any fun lately—purely and simply for the sake of having fun? Have you actively involved yourself in any new pursuit in the last year?

94. *Old habits can be broken! Yes, it is easier said than done. Does this mean it can't be done, or it isn't worth doing?*

95. *Are you aware that an attack of self-hate, punishment and guilt can be the first indication that you have broken a hidden contract with yourself?* You now have a chance to continue the self-beating—or—to look for the hidden contract and real freedom. I've had a number of women in treatment who became depressed every time they had sex. This reaction stopped after they "discovered" that they had hidden contracts to remain virgins.

96. *Do you realize that some people are physically promiscuous, but remain emotional virgins, giving nothing of their emotional selves to anybody?*

97. *Are you aware that relationships which become immediately sexual seldom become much more?* People who go right to bed somehow don't get to talk.

98. *Do you know that the ability to say "no" frees you to say "yes"?*

99. *Do you "inadvertently" make people an audience to your private battles?* They will seldom appreciate your need to act out domestic squabbles in their presence.

100. *Do presents, compliments, admiration, affection embarrass you?* Why can't you accept them graciously? Is this related to your lack of self-esteem? Have you checked your assets lately?

101. *Do you know that given half a chance, health is even more contagious than sickness?*

SECTION V

Help

Sometimes the going gets rough—rough enough, in fact, so that outside help is needed. Why suffer —let alone settle for being a loser?

This section is for you or anybody you are concerned about who needs help.

In this section, I want to discuss *when* help is necessary; *who is who* among the helpers; the *types of help* available, and the all-important *initial consultation*.

Read this section carefully; it can be very useful to anybody you wish to help now or in the future.

Your most important investment account

First, let's talk about economics—emotional economics.

To begin, I do not believe in a closed system of emotional energy. Unlike a bank account, I do not believe that a person has only so much love, so much hate and a fixed amount of energy to invest in himself or in others. In a relatively healthy person, emotional energy is not fixed, not measurable, and not depleted. In other words, an individual who is capable of love will not use up his supply of it. He can generate as much love as he wants without limit. His emotional economy is a healthy one. This is evidenced by ample and appropriate emotionale or feelings and fairly prudent emotional investments. Prudent investments are not made impulsively or compulsively. They are made spontaneously and carefully. The prudent investor gets to know, to really know, the person in whom he is investing. This always involves a relationship; he knows that relating takes time and he takes the time necessary to relate. He does not invest in destructive, spur-of-the-moment enterprises, driven by self-hate and a compulsive need to fail. He knows that it takes time to know the difference between casual acquaintanceships and maximum Max relationships. He trusts his feelings and especially those that come from deep down in the guts. But he has the capacity to wait for his feelings to evolve adequately before he commits them to a relating experience.

A sick economy, on the other hand, results in both poor production and poor investment. This kind of economy can freeze emotions, destroy flexibility and immobilize the production and projection of emotional energy or feelings. This results in overinvestments, underinvestments, inappropriate involvements and grievous disappointments. People in this kind of position have a propensity for making self-destructive relationships and a tendency for destroying potentially good relationships. They often feel that they have only a fixed, static amount of love or interest or involvement to bestow and that the rest of the world, including Max, operates in the same way. Thus, any interest Max may show in another person is felt as a deprivation of interest in one's self. These people feel that nobody could possibly want or accept (or reciprocate) their emotional investment, so why make it in the first place? The combination of feeling that one's emotional output is fixed and limited and that nobody really wants it anyway, plus the experience of having a history of disastrous relationships, inevitably results in relative or complete paralysis. I say "relative" because none of us relate to either ourselves or to others in a purely sick or healthy way. However, I am describing people here in whom sickness has crowded out health and in whom we see one or another neurotic symptom. These can run the gamut from much jealousy, envy, possessiveness, suspiciousness, etc., to severe anxiety, depression, withdrawal and even delusional and very irrational behavior. I do not wish to go into lengthy descriptions of human psychopathology here. Suffice it to say that people have problems. We all have them and we all have them all the time. For the most part, we can resolve them effectively ourselves. *But* if we can't, professional help is necessary. *Remember*—there can be no regeneration of emotionale unless effective emotional exchange takes place. Without communication, assets become frozen. Investments have stopped. Ownership of assets has been destroyed. Little emotion goes out and little emotion comes in. Emotional exchange has stopped, as well as emotional production. In short, an emotional economic breakdown has taken place. The individual can't feel clearly, can't make choices, decisions, changes, and he can't give or take. An outside expert must be called in—an emotional economist—*but* it is imperative, absolutely crucial, that the expert is, in fact, a real expert. He must help to get ownership back and to start the free flow of emotional exchange and generation going again.

Help!

All right, what about professional help? A process of real education in one's self is certainly interesting and valuable. Getting to know one's self deep down in one's guts can certainly make for growth and improved relating. But this process is very expensive in time, energy

251

and money, *and* there are simply not nearly enough *quali-fied* professionals available. So, I am really concerned here with those people who not only can use help, but who *need* help! I'm talking about those of us who are losers and who have been losers again and again. I'm talking about those of us who have not made it with Max and who have been unable to help ourselves. For those of us who are in serious emotional trouble, outside expert help is as necessary as it is for those suffering from heart, lung, kidney or other physical disabilities.

There are people who obviously need help. Their functioning in all areas of life has been severely curtailed. Their symptoms are often blatant and are organized into complicated patterns of behavior of long-standing dura-tion. These include phobias (inordinate and inappropriate fears, e.g., claustrophobia—fear of small shut-in places such as elevators, tunnels, trains, etc.), periodic depres-sions, anxiety attacks, psychosomatic disturbances, delu-sional beliefs, inappropriate and irrational behavior, etc. While these advanced conditions are certainly helped with proper treatment, it is much easier and more effec-tive to treat people before they develop chronic organized symptom complexes. Many people, fortunately, know that they are in serious trouble long before the more disturb-ing symptoms appear, let alone before these symptoms become solidified into chronic ways of life. There are those of us who may have suffered from impaired relating and functioning over extended periods of time, without overt evidence of more serious symptoms. There are those of us who, for a long time, have felt that things are just not right. We may have been suffering from subtle, but steadily increasing tension, moodiness, inability to con-centrate, increased feelings of apathy, loss of efficiency, increased anxiety, difficulty in making decisions, increased desire for seclusiveness, an increasing inability to relate on a serious level, inability to find a suitable sustained gainful occupation, an inability to sustain relationships with the opposite sex, a loss of intensity of feelings, appetites and desires, etc., etc. Early prophylactic help here may prevent more complicated and serious disturbances. *But* (and this is a giant one), people must be motivated to get something worthwhile from a treatment situation. Unfortunately, motivation, too, often comes only from the great suffering of more severe and advanced symptoms. Those who are fortunate enough to enter a necessary treatment situation early will find that less time, effort and pain will be involved in getting well.

What I am going to say now may sound strange, but believe me, it is important and born of much experience. *Be extremely wary of talking to the people at home (friends and relatives alike).* They can be helpful, but unfortunately they can also be quite destructive. Be ready for all kinds of undermining statements and DISREGARD THEM! Let me give you several *actual* examples: "All you have to do is just grab hold of yourself." "Why pay a psychiatrist? You can talk to me for nothing." "Look—just make up your mind—after all, it's only a question of willpower." "What you need is to get married." "You need a divorce." "What you need is a complete change—get another girl friend or change your job or sell your house or buy another car." "Some vitamin shots several times a week will fix you up." "Say—is there anybody crazy in your family?" (No family is exempt.) "A good love affair —that's what you need, a love affair." "Sex—SEX—that's what you need." "Just stop talking yourself into things." "Going to head-shrinkers is for kooks—know someone went for years—no help—I could tell—you know me, I know the score—besides you're not crazy, anyway." "Stay away from psychiatrists—they'll want to change you into someone else—wind up with a divorce or something."

"Work, work, work!" "Rest, rest, rest!" "Don't sleep—up and around—get up and go!" "So take a sleeping pill and get a good rest." "Ever hear of the new drug on TV—any drugstore." "So take a tranquilizer now and then." "What you ought to do is see a chiropractor." "Get yourself a good steam bath or a sauna and massages and take a vacation while you're at it—but forget your problems." "Have you thought about hypnosis?" "Exercise! I mean get out there and really knock yourself out and then sex —just work it off one way or the other." "Thought of doing something exciting—like buying something real crazy or going to the races or something?" "Getting to know yourself too well is dangerous—who needs it?" "Ever try Yoga?"

The fantastic thing is that the people making these statements actually feel that they are being helpful. It does not occur to them that they are something less than experts and are, in fact, projecting their own fears and conclusions regarding their own mental stability and foggy ideas about psychiatry. Of course, these ignorant and disturbed "well-wishers" are to be avoided. Unfortunately, people in emotional trouble are particularly suggestible, making them especially vulnerable to destructive possibilities. But, if they cannot be avoided, please be aware that they are expressing feelings about themselves vis-à-vis psychiatry and not about you. Most of these "well-wishers" are confusing psychiatry with mental illness. Let me explain how this unconscious illogical reasoning goes. Since being ill brings one to a psychiatrist, staying away from a psychiatrist will prevent mental illness. Like the proverbial ostrich, these people feel that prevention consists of denial, self-imposed blindness, ignorance and, if necessary, prejudice. (Please reread the "I don't believe in psychiatry muddle".) So, if you feel that you or yours need help, do indeed get it. *But* consult with an expert and *only* with an expert.

Who is who among the helpers?

Let us now discuss who the experts are—and aren't.

A *victim*—a potential patient who enters into treatment with a pseudotherapist, rather than with a qualified professional person. Although he may pay a lot of money for "treatment" and keep his appointments faithfully, he has destructively entered into an unrewarding, and even dangerous, situation. This occurs all too often and even when the patient is not too sick to investigate for himself.

A *patient*—anybody who feels that he may profit from help, and goes about getting it knowledgeably. If he becomes involved in legitimate and appropriate treatment with a qualified person, he has taken the first step toward improving his situation and making it with Max.

The therapist—used in the broadest sense, this may apply to any person who is involved in a therapeutic relationship with the patient. Thus, a friend, a relative, a teacher, or a medical doctor, who directly or indirectly helps the patient, may be called a therapist. Anybody who temporarily eases the burden may be said to fall into this category. Of course, the help derived from this kind of relationship does not solve problems on a deeper or a sustained level. *Our* chief concern in this section is, of course, the therapist who functions in a completely professional capacity. Remember please! Most states of the United States have no laws to prevent people from going into the "psychotherapy business." Consequently, we see people with highly varied background and training or no training, dispensing a vast variety of "therapy" without being qualified to do so, even in the very least. These "therapists" or "psychotherapists" or "counselors" or "advisors," etc., generally fall into one of three categories, all to be scrupulously avoided.

1) *The out-and-out charlatans.* These people "practice" everything from anxiety-reducing massages to black magic. They are not at all adverse to advertising in telephone books, newspapers, circulars, by mail or in cheap magazines. In some states, they print their names and claims on the sides of buildings. Some use tactics not unlike the medicine man of old, who furnished a cure-all elixir and a dose of entertainment for good measure. Many of these people do not seem to mind an occasional brush with the law, sometimes resulting from prescribing or issuing drugs with which they are totally unfamiliar, without a license. Some have been known to operate blackmail and con-game enterprises. Some engage in exotic forms of sexually stimulating treatments, which are not specifically prohibited by law. I know of one woman whose former "therapist" *treated her* by breast massage.

2) *The nonprofessional therapist.* People in this category are often well educated and sometimes even well meaning, but untrained in the practice of psychiatry. Some of them may have been patients in treatment themselves and so gained the notion that they could function as therapists. They may be teachers, lawyers or members of any other honored profession, who consider their own experiences as patients to be ample specialty training to qualify them for a psychotherapeutic practice. Others have not even had the benefit of their own treatment. None has been well analyzed. It is to be expected that a well-analyzed person has a good sense of personal and

professional identification and therefore would not attempt to perform in an area in which he is insufficiently trained. I recall a lawyer who talked a few clients out of divorce, graduated himself to the role of marriage counselor and then took the next easy step to the practice of psychotherapy. If this sounds shocking, consider that most people do not hesitate to become involved in technical discussions involving human behavior, psychology and psychiatry. The very same people who would never venture any opinion in any other highly technical area (e.g., internal medicine, cardiology, surgery, quantum mechanics, electrical engineering, etc.) enter—unabashed and with complete abandon—into "discussions" with professionally trained people. Possibly some of us consider that daily living and resolving conflicts and emotions give expertise in this area—BUT THEY DON'T! Of course, what makes it possible is the fact that the discussion can proceed without knowledge of too many technical terms—each person may become a self-appointed expert. I have been witness to many incidents in which untrained people argue quite vehemently (and arrogantly) about various aspects of the highly technical specialty of psychiatry without quite realizing that the psychiatrist has spent years in the complex study of human behavior. Please note that the self-styled experts are often victimized by other self-styled experts when they themselves need help.

3) *The unqualified professionals.* These are workers in psychiatry or related fields whose training does not qualify them for giving psychotherapy, but who nevertheless assume the work of therapist. This includes social workers, psychologists and psychiatrists, who have been trained in their respective fields, but who have not had the special training necessary for therapeutic work.

Well, who is the trained therapist? We may rightly call those people therapists who are trained to give guidance or supportive treatment in some area such as marriage or vocation. Since guidance is a form of therapy, we may consider qualified social workers, psychiatrists, teachers, or lawyers "limited therapists" who have been trained to do this work. Therapy here, however, is not based on psychoanalytic principles. It takes place on a limited scale and on a relatively superficial level. It does not and should not deal with unconscious processes, since the exploration of such processes is highly specialized and complex.

Therapy, on a deeper level, based on psychoanalytic concepts and dynamics involving exploration of unconscious processes, should only be practiced by highly trained psychotherapists. These are psychiatrists who have completed psychiatric residencies and training in accredited psychoanalytic institutes.

Many other people perform in vital capacities in psychiatry and its allied fields. There are numerous trained specialists including occupational therapists, school guidance counselors, occupational counselors, sociologists, anthropologists, biochemical researchers, attendants, psychiatric nurses, teachers of disturbed adults, teachers of brain-damaged adults, teachers of mentally retarded adults and children, etc. At this point, I will describe several categories of workers in the very center of the field, whose roles are sometimes confused.

The psychologist operates in several different branches of psychology. He is specifically trained in each to perform a specific and important job.

The social psychologist is a person trained to observe and understand human behavior as it relates to social phenomenon. He may be interested in the psychology of war, in the psychology of crowds, or in other mass phenomena. He may conduct polls of public opinion and utilize other research procedures in making valid and useful determinations.

The experimental psychologist does research on human behavioral phenomena as evidenced by the individual or by groups of people. He possesses a basic fund of knowledge about human physiology, since this is essential to the experiments which he conducts. He is concerned with such phenomena as the conditioned reflex, man's behavior in isolation, man's use of his senses in perception, etc.

The clinical psychologist is usually a Ph.D. (not an M.D.) who majored in psychology as an undergraduate. He then went on to advanced studies in psychology on the graduate level. In earning his graduate degrees (master's and doctorate) he masters theories of education, testing, learning and behavior. He is now usually required to serve an "internship" (nonmedical) on the psychiatric service of a qualified hospital either as an integrated part of his graduate program or after he has received a graduate degree. In most hospital programs, he receives further training and experience in testing patients. He usually administers and evaluates IQ tests and projective psychological tests, such as the Rorschach (ink blot), Thematic Apperception Test and others. The tests and their psychological interpretations can be used by the psychiatrist in the evaluation of the patient's mental condition. Some programs also permit supervised treatment of patients in psychotherapy. The clinical psychologist may or may not be analyzed himself. If he has enrolled in a program which includes some psychotherapeutic training, personal analysis is apt to be strongly recommended; otherwise it is usually optional. Clinical psychologists are eminently qualified to do research in the area of psychodynamics. Their contribution in the field is notable. There are currently several nonmedical institutes which train psychologists to do analytic work.

The social worker ordinarily majors in some branch of the social sciences, such as psychology, anthropology or sociology in undergraduate school. As part of the master's degree program, he does field work and spends time working in a social service agency. There are three general divisions of social work: *case work, group work* and *psychiatric social work*. The *case worker* is employed by a social service agency and is assigned "clients." These clients are people in need of assistance and the case worker helps them get it—whether it be medical, psychiatric, or economic. He may undertake counseling therapy when necessary and appropriate. The *group worker* is usually assigned to a settlement house or Y.M.C.A., or to a Youth Board. He works with groups of underprivileged children or young people or old people (Golden Age Groups). The *psychiatric social worker* is trained in a psychiatric institution beyond his college B.A. and his graduate M.A. studies in social work. He works on the psychiatric staff of a hospital or clinic. It is his job to prepare the family to receive the patient discharged from an institution. He also finds foster homes for needy children and locates and investigates institutions for disturbed children. It is useful, but not mandatory, for the psychiatric social worker to undergo analysis himself.

The psychiatrist. First, let me say that the psychiatrist, analyst or therapist is a human being. This may seem to be obvious, but consider that the public image of the psychiatrist is often strange, to say the least. A psychiatrist has no special powers; he is not a mind reader; and he does not deal in the mysteries of black magic. He works in an office and he has a demanding job. It would be better if he were neither damned nor idolized, as he so often is. He has both the assets and limitations inherent in being human. In the best instances, he has sensitivity, humility and talent, as well as good training in his field.

All psychiatrists are physicians, medical doctors. They follow the course of study of all other medical doctors. As a premedical student, a young man may earn either a B.A. or B.S. degree as preparation for medical school. After he has been graduated from an accredited medical school, he completes an internship in a hospital for either one or two years. Upon completion of his internship and licensing examinations by the state of his choice, the future psychiatrist goes through specialty training. This training is parallel to the training of other medical specialists, such as obstetricians, pediatricians, surgeons, internists, etc.

Psychiatric training consists of three years residency in either a psychiatric hospital or the psychiatric service of a large general hospital. The hospital must be accredited by the American Board of Psychiatry. During his residency, the doctor (resident psychiatrist in training) interviews patients, writes up case histories and eventually learns to make decisions and recommendations for admission, continued hospitalization or discharge of patients. He attends lectures and seminars on diagnostic techniques and in some residencies, on the dynamics of human behavior and pathology. He also may work in an out-patient clinic in his last year. If so, he does some psychotherapy under the supervision of an experienced attending psychiatrist. The resident psychiatrist eventually is in charge of large groups of patients. It is his duty to integrate the work of nurses, attendants, psychologists and social workers. He studies and works with various physiological modalities, such as electroconvulsive treatment, and insulin coma treatment, in order to learn their indications and usage. He may eventually be called upon to render expertise to the courts for state hospital commitments.

His own personal analysis is optional unless he is in a psychoanalytically integrated psychiatric residency, which is becoming more common.

Upon completion of his residency, he is a psychiatrist. This means that he can make a psychiatric examination, evaluation and diagnosis. He will have a good concept of prognosis (outcome in particular cases). He will know how to administer physiological treatment (E.C.T. —Electroshock treatment and drugs) and will sometimes function as a limited supportive therapist. He may work in a hospital or clinic or engage in private practice.

There are several psychiatric specialties (specialties within a specialty) and some men function in a combination of these capacities.

The child psychiatrist—In addition to the general psychiatric training I describe above, the child psychiatrist serves an extra two years of residency on a child service (for disturbed children). Most of his practice will be devoted to the care of children, though some child psychiatrists also work with the parents of disturbed children. The role of the child psychiatrist is particularly exacting and requires particular talents of heart and mind. It is necessary for a doctor in this subspecialty to possess the special qualities which make it possible for him to function well with children. No amount of training can make up for a lack of this gift. Extreme sensitivity is a prime requisite in communicating with disturbed youngsters, who sometimes cannot make themselves understood in any ordinary language or symbols. The ideal child psychiatrist has a combination of an extraordinary gift of sensitivity and the best in psychiatric, as well as psychoanalytic, training.

The group therapist—While the group therapist is

ideally a psychiatrist trained in psychoanalysis, he may also be a psychologist or social worker trained in group dynamics and supervised by a psychiatrist. The therapist here treats a group of patients (four to twelve) all at the same time. One of the valuable techniques is to make use of transference relationships between members of the groups, as well as between patients and therapist. People have a way of recapitulating their own family relationships in the group, thus revealing their problems in family as well as other relationships. This gives an excellent opportunity for insight into relating difficulties as well as practice in healthier relating. Much, however, depends on the insight and skill of the professional expert in charge.

Some people find a one-to-one relationship (individual therapy) too threatening and pressing. They can only take the dilution of a group. Others find great support in the firsthand knowledge that other people share similar problems. Others need the concrete relating workouts found in a group to work out their own relating problems. Group therapy is of particular value to those people who are also in individual treatment or who have been in individual treatment. *But* group therapy can be useless and destructive unless conducted by an expert. Only an expert can choose people who will work together in a mutually constructive enterprise. Only an expert can see to it that the group does, in fact, gain maximally from the group experience.

The psychoanalyst or psychoanalytic therapist—It was formerly the practice to offer psychoanalytic training to both medical and lay (nonmedical) people. At present, the well-established, highly qualified institutes accept only medical doctors. However, there has been a recent movement to reestablish institutes for the training of nonmedical psychoanalysts. The William Alanson White Institute of Psychiatry, Psychoanalysis and Psychology in

New York is exceptional in that it trains psychologists as well as medical people to be psychoanalysts. This institute trains a few highly qualified teachers and social workers to help them in special work, but does not train them to be practicing psychoanalysts.

There are two official national psychoanalytic organizations. The American Psychoanalytic Association is the older of the two. It accepts only graduates of the Freudian institutes such as the New York Psychoanalytic Institute, the Columbia (University) Institute, the Brooklyn Institute and several others in the large cities of the United States. The second organization is the more recently organized American Academy of Psychoanalysis, whose members are graduates of all qualified schools (Freudian and non-Freudian). This organization tries to facilitate better communication among the various psychoanalytic schools of various theoretical persuasions. Thus, Freudians may come in contact with neo-Freudians, such as graduates of the American Institute of Psychoanalysis, which largely follows the work of Karen Horney. Or they may exchange ideas with graduates of the Comprehensive Course in Psychoanalysis of the New York Medical College, an eclectic school (encompassing all theories) or the William Alanson White Institute of Psychiatry, Psychoanalysis and Psychology, largely influenced by the work of the late Harry Stack Sullivan. If you are interested in the different theories of psychoanalysis, I suggest you read Karen Horney's *New Ways in Psychoanalysis* (1933) and Ruth Monroe's *Schools of Analytic Thought*.

Regardless of the school, the training of a psychoanalyst is rigorous and intensive. Only about 15 percent of all psychiatrists are actually psychoanalysts with specialized training by an institute, qualified by the two major organizations. Thus, you can readily see that to use the term psychiatrist as being all-inclusive is very inaccurate. Admission to the various institutes is highly selective and unlikely candidates are carefully screened and weeded out along the way. The potential candidate must undergo a series of three or more interviews with faculty members of the institute. He may also be required to take a complete battery of psychological tests. Applicants are expected to have completed two years of their three-year psychiatric training before beginning psychoanalytic training. Many candidates do not begin training until they have completed their psychiatric residencies. Psychoanalytic training, then, may be considered post-graduate to psychiatric training.

During training, the future analyst goes through complete personal psychoanalytic treatment, for which he pays the regular fees. He attends classes on the various aspects of psychoanalytic theory and technique: workshops on dreams, clinical conferences, continuous case seminars, reading courses in theory and workshops on human behavior. He is expected to attend accessible professional meetings, where papers are read and discussed. Finally, he works with at least three different patients in the actual treatment situation of analysis, under the supervision of a different psychoanalyst for each patient.

The fully qualified psychoanalyst has completed the necessary courses, supervised analysis and his own personal analysis. His personal analysis is extremely important and must be exceedingly thorough. If it isn't, the analyst's future work will tend to bring out his own neurotic residuals. A thorough analysis will help him to help his patients to the greatest degree without blockage by personal impediments. Therefore, a "training analysis," though it is similar to other analysis in all other ways, is sometimes of longer duration.

The graduate or certified analyst usually retains his connection with his training institute. The latter furnishes

265

a center for lectures, presentation of papers and a general forum for the exchange of ideas and information. Some psychoanalysts eventually become faculty members and supervising analysts at the institute, thus passing on their acquired knowledge and training to other psychiatrists who wish to become analysts.

Relating and relating treatment

What about the kinds of help available? Let's first talk about relating as it applies to the treatment situation and then let's try to shed some light on psychoanalytic treatment. From there, we will go on to some of the other kinds of help.

Again and again I hear people ask, "How can talk treatments help me?" Relating either in or out of a treatment situation consists of much more than verbal communication. I've said some of what I am going to say now earlier, but I think that it is worth our while to go over it in this particular context once again.

What does an individual bring into a relationship? He brings his body, his feelings, his attitudes, his values, his health, his sickness, his ideas and his words. In short, he brings himself. He communicates at least part of himself to the other individual and responds to what the other individual communicates to him. There are also parts of himself that are hidden—hidden from others and even from himself. There are attitudes and emotions that look obvious superficially but which on a deeper level can at times be quite devious. What goes on between people is relating (and of course, this exchange exists in all kinds of qualities). *But* relating goes on even when a person is alone. It goes on because his feelings go on—and his feelings always involve other individuals and objects and himself, and so he relates to people, objects, and himself. This relating does not remain in a pat or static pattern. Diverse ways of feeling and emoting and fluctuations in intensity of feeling (feelings of love, hate, etc.) constantly take place. This is especially true when a person is healthy enough to be spontaneous, that is, to be free in the way that he feels and to have freedom of choice in his actions. However (as described earlier), spontaneity is sometimes lost and patterns of behavior become more or less fixed. Here, the *victim* suffers from enough anxiety so that his life (without his awareness) has been reduced to a rigid pattern designed to mitigate his anxiety and leave little or no freedom for anything else. Thus, we are dealing with a person whose relating is patterned on making him feel safe. Of course, these patterns are highly varied and sometimes are quite subtle and devious.

As an example, a man may have developed a neurotic behavior pattern in which he feels safe only when he feels that he is liked. Therefore, his relating may mainly consist of constant attempts to get people to like him. This pattern will involve many checks and blocks on his emotions and be sure that he will suffer from many, many muddles. This man may not be able to express anger lest he in turn incurs anger, thus threatening his constantly being liked position. The pattern, once established, is not only extremely tenacious, set, compulsive, but may also be relatively hidden by rationalizations such as, "Oh, I don't really care about being liked—just happens, I'm very likable." Of course, a price is paid for the repression of emotions, however effective the rationalization may be. Anger, held back, must be expressed somehow. Felt as other than anger, it can lead to one whale of a headache both figuratively and literally. This, of course, is only one small detail of an intricate neurotic pattern. This pattern, designed to defend against the discomfort of anxiety—but inherent in itself, contains and generates much anxiety and has a crippling effect on the individual and his ability to relate.

Many relationships are anything but therapeutic. Some of them are downright destructive. However, there are instances when relating can make a person feel better. A friend gives some kind encouragement demonstrating that she cares; just being with somebody one likes; letting go of some pent-up emotion in getting angry at a trusted, nonvindictive friend; relating to an object—as when a purchase has a cheering effect. Of course, this kind of help does not make for "insight" and is therefore usually temporary. However, there are therapists whose professional technique largely consists of this type of treatment or a combination of them. Treatment of this type is often called the common-sense approach. Various therapies and terms for them are as follows: *ventilation*—encouraging the patient to talk out his problem; *abreaction*—encouraging the patient to emote his pent-up feelings; *psychodrama*—in which the patient acts out his difficulties; *counseling,* especially marriage counseling; *guidance therapy; supportive therapy; work therapy;* hypnosis (valuable only in highly selected cases as an adjunct in finding certain hidden factors).

Now, what methods exist to help people in need on a deeper, more permanent level? How can we expose, examine and change a neurotic way of relating to effect a healthier ability to relate? The most effective means known to date is a relating therapy called psychoanalysis or psychoanalytic psychotherapy. This treatment depends mainly upon basic concepts introduced by Sigmund

Freud. An individual's neurotic attitudes—his way of relating—are consistent, regardless of whom he is relating
to. Oh, yes, there will be what appear to be superficial
differences, but basic qualities will remain the same regardless of whom he is relating to. If he is possessive,
self-effacing, envious, fearful, dependent, arrogant, then
he will be so, regardless of who it is he is relating to. Now,
this is true of his relationship with his psychotherapist, a
man trained to examine and understand the full anatomy
of relating. The relationship between the analyst and the
patient becomes a special area where neurotic trends can
be exposed, can be examined and can be changed. It is
that rare place where the patient has the opportunity to
be as irrational as he feels. This is the place where he can
examine the patterns, origins and effects of his irrationalities. This is the place where he can learn and practice
healthier ways of life, leading to a diminishing compulsiv-
ity and a growth of spontaneity and freedom of choice.

Psychoanalysis

Now, let's talk about psychoanalysis or analysis or psychoanalytic psychotherapy (therapy based on
analytic principles but not as intense or lengthy).

Psychoanalysis is the most important form of relating
therapy in the psychoanalytically trained psychiatrist's
medical bag. This treatment includes ventilation, abreaction and support. But the latter activities are not what
makes psychoanalysis the deeper treatment that it is. In
order to more clearly understand what goes on in psycho-

analysis, we must have familiarity with five of its basic tenets as introduced by Sigmund Freud:

1) *Psychic determinism, or unconscious determinism:* The meaning of this term is extremely important. It alludes to the fact that psychological phenomena, all thoughts, every action, all behavior, are determined. What does determined mean? It means that no thought is accidental and that no action is meaningless. A thought, any thought, every thought, has meaning and is part of a large pattern of thinking and feeling, characteristic of the individual in question. The meaning of many thoughts, fantasies, dreams, and actions may not be obvious at first inspection, but ultimate study will reveal the meaning of each symbol formation, and that is what a thought is— a symbol—a symbol of what is going on in a human being. That something may be relatively apparent or hidden and is often deeply buried in the unconscious. Some symbols have several meanings on different levels. In any case, while the thought or fantasy or other manifestation may not make apparent sense at first, careful, skilled and experienced probing will eventually decodify it.

As an example, let us at this point take a look at a very prevalent manifestation, namely having "peculiar thoughts." People have them and they worry about them. Some are terrified by them and many others of us are ashamed to talk about them. These are some of the statements I've heard regarding "peculiar thoughts":

"Am I crazy?"

"Does this mean that I'm a potential rapist or pervert?"

"Could I become a murderer and actually do such terrible things?"

"Will I lose my memory or my ability to think straight?"

270

"Will I suddenly jump or scream or commit some other ridiculous act?"

"Do these crazy fantasies mean that I can lose control completely and just run amok?"

Odd thoughts for the most part fall into one or both of two categories. They may be odd because of their inappropriate timing or by virtue of their content. For example, a grocery clerk is adding up a column of figures and suddenly the word (or thought) "bougainvillea" pops into his head. Bougainvillea is a plant that grows in California and there is nothing odd about it. What is odd is the timing—the popping up of the word seemingly out of context—while adding up figures. Now, let's look at an example of a thought peculiar because of its content. A man walks across the street with a friend and suddenly a visual thought (or fantasy) occurs to him. In his mind's eye, he sees a gory sight indeed: a passing truck decapitates his friend whose bloody head is now rolling along in the gutter. This "thought" is obviously gory and bizarre enough to justify its being called "peculiar."

If we evaluate thoughts in terms of morality (is it a good thought or is it a bad thought), it will be impossible to understand them on a constructive level. The good/bad, smart/stupid, normal/crazy approach kills off the possibility of getting to know ourselves better, let alone the possibility of growth.

How do we approach "thoughts" analytically—that is, as meaningful symbols?

The first step is acceptance. If we accept a thought, however bizarre, as our very own, without self-hate or self-chastisement, without guilt, but with full responsibility and openness and healthy curiosity, only then are we ready to understand and to make use of it.

The next step is one that I discussed in the section on muddles. I repeat it here because it is all-important in this particular context—it is crucial that one realize that a thought is not an action! Only a minute percentage of thoughts are translated into action. Most thoughts are simply set aside, discarded. Some, especially peculiar thoughts, could be very useful in extending knowledge of ourselves. For this to happen, however, it must be realized that a thought is never an accident. It always has meaning. *But* a thought, especially a peculiar one, very often has a meaning which is not at first apparent and is often far removed from what appears to be its obvious meaning. Each word or symbol has a special meaning depending on the person using the particular symbol. Let's take our examples:

The word bougainvillea "inappropriately" popped into our grocery clerk's mind. Let us assume that the clerk now associates freely, that is, he allows other words to come to mind freely. It becomes apparent that the clerk once lived in California (bougainvillea is a plant that grows in California) and he soon associates and connects the word bougainvillea with California. It turns out that while adding figures he had a sudden urge, desire and preference to be in sunny California. That feeling led to the thought—bougainvillea—an exotic symbol which at once brought on the feelings, odors and feel of California. Bougainvillea, to him, represented the antithesis of the grocery store and the place in which he most desired to be.

Now, you may ask, "Why couldn't the clerk just say, 'I'd like to be in a nice place rather than in this grocery store'? Why couldn't the other fellow who saw his friend dead just say that he was angry—if not to his friend, at least to himself?" The answers to the latter questions are complicated. Suffice it to say that when a given feeling cannot be tolerated by an individual (let us say that our grocery clerk has an idealized version of total dedication to duty and that the other man cannot tolerate the idea of generating anger) and he sits on that feeling and attempts to squelch it, it tends to snowball and grow in intensity, so that when it finally surfaces, it often comes through with great exaggeration and distortion. If the man crossing the street feels that he must not get angry at friends, his repressed irritation can grow and grow until a final stimulating situation (an irritating remark by the friend) can bring forth a much exaggerated murderous symbol. *But* this thought is not an *actuality* nor is it directly representative of an actuality. It is a symbol and it symbolizes the original small (but unfortunately repressed) irritation.

Before I leave the subject of peculiar thoughts and psychic determinism, I want to mention a very common, but distressing type of thought. I call this the self-ridiculing thought. It usually involves someone suddenly seeing himself doing something crazy like running through a quiet library screaming or running through a train berserk. More often than not, this kind of thought can be traced to a sudden feeling of self-contempt. I remember a patient who always had these thoughts on trains going to look for work which she felt was below her station in life. If you have a thought like this, it may be valuable to ask yourself—why am I angry with me? Why do I look upon myself with disfavor?

As for going crazy, an individual who can discern the fact that a thought is peculiar is very far from crazy. As such, there is little chance indeed that a thought will become an impulsive action. An individual may not be able to control his thoughts, but he may still do an excellent job in having a choice over his actions.

There are conditions in which bizarre thoughts are continuous and very complicated. In some cases these thoughts are repeated again and again in an obsessive

273

way. This symptom may be indicative of a deep-seated conflict for which psychoanalytic psychotherapy is indicated.

Now let's get on to the second important tenet of psychoanalysis.

2) *Transference:* This is the term used to express what goes on in that all-important relating process between patient and therapist. Freud felt that the patient transfers his feelings and attitudes, particularly his early infantile patterns of behavior toward his parents, to his therapist. This transfer of feelings (unconscious) contains the neurotic attitudes of the patient and the term *transference neurosis* was coined. Later workers, particularly Karen Horney and her followers, felt that the patient transfers healthy as well as neurotic or sick attitudes to the therapist. Thus, the transference or relationship in the analytic situation affords the possibility of examining neurotic constellations and also of exploring and owning seeds of health. Regardless of the controversy regarding Freud's transference phenomena, all of the schools of psychoanalysis accept the concept of transference as one of utmost importance as a therapeutic tool. There is no doubt that an analytic examination of the patient's relationship to his therapist is most revealing and leads to the possibility of resolving problems in the service of healthy growth.

3) *Dreams* and the importance of their interpretation in analytic treatment form the third tenet of psychoanalysis. It is not surprising that Freud called the dream the "royal road to the unconscious." Through the interpretation of dreams, one can learn much about an individual's unconscious (much of the stuff that he is not aware of but which make him tick) and character structure and his ways of relating to people. However, the interpretation of dreams is not a simple business. A dream

can only be understood by understanding the symbols of the dreamer, that is, by understanding much about the dreamer himself. The main instrument used in decoding a dream is *free association*. The associations (thoughts or fantasies brought up at random without regard for logic or meaning) the patient produces regarding the dream material will lead to an understanding of the dream itself. Now, Freud pointed out that a dream has manifest and latent or deeper meaning. It is only by understanding the symbols of the dreamer that we can arrive at the latent (hidden and deeper) content of the dream. Freud felt that the latent content always involves a wish fulfillment —something the dreamer wishes to come true, but which he cannot reveal openly to himself for fear of great guilt, self-contempt and self-derogation and possible chastisement by one's self and others (Mama, Papa and society). For example, Mrs. Smith described a harrowing dream in which she lost her three-year-old daughter and further describes the anguish and suffering she felt during the dream. She spends the rest of the analytic hour describing her difficulty with her daughter, including bed-wetting, colds and sleepless nights. At the end of the hour, she remembers the dream again and says, "I would feel terrible if I lost her."

The manifest content of the dream reveals much fear, grief, and trepidation over the loss of the dreamer's child. But the latent content actually reveals a desire to lose her (at least temporarily), perhaps linked to repressed anger at her. This may be due to the bed-wetting and other problems of which Mrs. Smith would like to be relieved and free. This anger and desire for freedom from parental responsibility may also be linked to other aspects of Mrs. Smith's life (not revealed here) and especially to her own life as a child and her relationship with her own mother.

4) *Free association:* Freud discovered that if a per-

son sat back, or better yet, lay back on a couch (with minimum interference from the therapist) and said anything that came to mind regardless of apparent meaning, lack of meaning, connectedness or unconnectedness, a very special pattern emerged. This pattern inevitably reveals a great deal about the individual in question and how he relates to himself and other people. However, the individual is unaware (unconscious) of much that emerges until it is interpreted to him and put together by the experienced analyst. Thoughts, fantasies and particularly "peculiar thoughts" turn out to be a treasure house of formerly hidden insights. These make maximum sense, as they are studied, as part of the individual's total history and life processes.

5) *The role of sex:* There has been considerable controversy about the role of sex in psychic life, among the various schools of psychoanalysis. This is especially true of Freud's concept of infantile sexuality (that children experience sexual feelings, desires, frustrations, long before puberty) as well as his stress on the importance of oedipal feelings (sexual fixations of children on parents). It is also true of his notion of the existence of latent homosexuality in all human beings. A major controversy rages over his concept that all neurotic difficulties can ultimately be attributed to early sexual problems. Many workers, especially the followers of Karen Horney, feel that just the contrary is true. Sexual difficulties are ever present in neurosis, but only as a result of, and a concomitant of neurotic relating difficulties. In any case, Freud must be credited with the elucidation of the importance of the role of sex in psychopathology. As I've said before, since the sexual relationship potentially represents the closest relationship of all, it is not difficult to envision this area as one of great importance in neurotic manifestations.

276

Now, what about early memories? This, too, is a somewhat controversial area. All schools do, however, feel that early memories are important as points of early trauma and repressed material and undoubtedly play a large role in understanding the origin of many present difficulties. Unlike the movie version, however, psychoanalysis does not consist of ferreting out the one or two traumatic incidents in a patient's life and thereby curing him. On the contrary, psychoanalysis, at best, is a painstaking, difficult treatment necessitating much work on the part of the patient and the therapist. The work involves a meticulous examination and reevaluation of all of the patient's attitudes and emotions and his ways of relating to himself and the rest of the world. This is not a guidance treatment and it is certainly not the goal of treatment to make the patient over in the image of his analyst. On the contrary, the therapist offers no advice, no guidance. He serves to uncover and interprets in order to clarify, but it is the patient who must use his newfound knowledge of himself to make decisions and to act in his own behalf. The process is much more than an intellectual experience. Intellectual understanding can be helpful (if not used to convert the analytic situation into a classroom device designed to resist treatment and change). To be really effective, the process must be an emotional one—a feeling examination of feelings, a feeling understanding of feelings and eventually, a feeling change of feelings. In analysis "why" is unimportant and "what, how and when?" are very important.

An extremely important goal in analysis is to educate the individual in himself and to make him acceptable to himself (as he actually is minus the illusions). This makes healthy growth possible. If treatment is successful and healthy growth initiated, both patient and doctor will have gained understanding in this relating treatment.

Psychoanalytic insight

I discussed "insight" in describing the difference between insight and willpower in the section on muddles. I will repeat aspects of that discussion here, but please bear with me. I feel that this concept is so important that repetition is justified in this particular context (treatment).

In the section Muddles, I spoke of "Knowing and Knowing." A very deep form of knowing is "insight." I use the word insight here in a very special way. I use it as applied to psychoanalysis which, in addition to being known as a relating therapy, is also sometimes called an insight therapy.

In the last chapter, I wrote, "a feeling explanation of feeling, and a feeling understanding of feeling, and a feeling change of feeling." Now, what I was talking about there was insight. By insight, I mean a special kind of understanding—an understanding on a level deeper than knowing, deeper than the understanding of logic, deeper than intellectual know-how. I speak of understanding on an emotional level. But this is just another way of saying insight. What does insight actually mean and why is it so important? It is an emotional understanding of emotions or the process of feeling of and about feelings. It is the know-how which reaches down into the unconscious, stirs it up, lights up dark corners, brings old feelings to the surface of consciousness which hook up to new feelings. Now, these feelings, altogether, may produce a sensation of awareness and insight, which can lead to hopefulness and the freedom to live and blossom into growth.

Perhaps this sounds like an attempt at a poetic explanation. But there is poetry in insight—just as there is in the living of life itself.

Now, my explanation must be limited, since I am using words to describe an entity which is primarily involved with feeling, and which must be *felt* to be fully appreciated. However, since this insight business is so important, I shall try another route—an analogy—at best, second best, but here perhaps, best.

Let's talk once again about the chow mein example that I spoke about in the section on muddles. We can talk about the taste of chow mein, and without tasting it, understand about its taste intellectually. We can discuss its consistency and its chemistry. We can compare it with other foods and foods in general that look alike. Through this discussion, we may be able to evolve a pattern of ideas representing the taste of chow mein, and through this representative pattern, we may even feel certain ways about the stuff. It may seem appetizing or nauseating, tempting or repulsive. But, all this understanding of chow mein, even when we have feelings about it, will still not produce anything much deeper than an intellectual, reasoning kind of understanding. Since we have not tasted the stuff, we cannot incorporate this taste and cannot integrate it with our other taste experiences. We cannot relate it to the large general body of all our experiences (unconscious and conscious). Now assume that we have at one time eaten chow mein and that the experience, the taste, has become part of the whole, part of all that goes on in us. But assume also that a prohibition relating to the eating of certain foods, including Chinese food, exists. As a result, the experience is repressed, dimmed, and even blotted out. Now, talk about chow mein will be just that, talk; an analytic discussion may lead to intellectual understanding, but little else. However, let us assume that through the process of free association, and the newfound strength arrived at through the analytic relationship, plus the analytic interpretations and elucidations thereof; our feeling of chow mein, plus the early memory of its taste is brought to light. In addition, the early prohibitions concerning Chinese foods and the present feeling of censorship are not only brought to light, but analyzed completely, including the anger, hates, etc., involved in the necessities for prohibitions of this kind, etc. Then the taste of the chow mein and much of the feeling involved with it may suddenly be brought to light.

Now, assume that we are not dealing with chow mein, but rather with attitudes toward and feelings about it, that is, with a reaction pattern, a way of behaving. If through the experiences between analyst and analysand (person being analyzed) and through the interpretations of the analyst, the patient feels the illumination and integration of the attitude in question, we can then say he has insight.

How does this "insight" help in analytic treatment? First, when a correct interpretation is made, leading to insight, there is immediately great supportive value. This is not the superficial support of reassurance (you'll be all right, just don't worry, etc.). It is a more profound support, gleaned from the recognition of understanding from another human being. And it is also support derived from the beginnings of knowledge of one's difficulties which is the first step toward solution of those difficulties, the first step away from hopelessness. I am again reminded of someone who has a severe allergy, but doesn't know to what he is allergic. The great trick here is in finding the allergen. After much testing and suffering, he finds out that the offending substance is banana. Knowing the allergen and his reaction to it, he will, in the future, avoid bananas. In analysis, through many, many insights the patient becomes aware of the poor economy of his neurotic patterns. Through his newfound awareness, and with work, change to a better emotional economy can be initiated. In short, however distasteful the truth may be, and quite often the undistorted truth is not distasteful at all, it leads to hope because it is the beginning of constructive understanding and changes.

Surgery, E.C.T. and drugs

Brain surgery today is generally confined to organic diseases of the brain (brain tumors, etc., as differentiated from mental illness). For a while "psychosurgery" (lobotomy, lobectomy) was used and is occasionally still used in a heroic effort to remedy long-standing, seemingly incurable mental illness. This treatment has largely been abandoned since it has many drawbacks, including only a haphazard chance at sustained improvement. My own feeling is that a normal physiology and chemistry can produce both a healthy and sick psyche. I feel that a surgical approach is a primitive and oversimplified one at best. People get very sick mentally because of very sick early relationships and it is relating therapy which holds the best hope for getting well. I am not speaking of organic brain disease or congenital deficit of any kind. Physiological, surgical and chemical approaches are definitely in order where there is evidence of physiological disorder. To date, there is no concrete conclusive evidence of abnormal brain function (chemically or physically) in the common mental illnesses, let alone the less serious emotional disorders (neuroses).

Electroshock treatment (also known as electroconvulsive treatment) can be very useful if used where necessary and with great prudence and skill. This treatment is indicated and can even be life-saving in conditions where the patient cannot be helped sufficiently by drugs or reached by psychotherapy. This is true of very severe depressions and of very severe withdrawal reactions. Since E.C.T. does not give "insight" or change an individual's basic pattern of behaving and relating to himself or to others, it cannot effect a "cure" or great personality improvement or growth. Used judiciously, it can ease symptoms sufficiently so that psychotherapy and insight can progress toward more ambitious goals. I do feel the E.C.T. is sometimes used injudiciously, that is, where it is not indicated and that it is overused in certain quarters. The best protection against inappropriate treatment, in any medical area, is proper consultation. More about that later.

To date, there has been no drug discovered that "cures" or gives wisdom or gives growth or insight. The "old drugs"—insulin and Metrazol—are still used in severe emotional disturbance, but much less so than in the past. They must be used most carefully and only in a controlled hospital setting.

The "old drugs"—sedatives and hypnotics, including barbiturates and narcotics—are still used in the treatment of emotional disturbances, but also not as much as in the past. They can be very useful in expert hands as relievers of symptoms. They are never cures, and again much prudence must be exercised by the physician in charge, since habit or addiction is a possibility.

The "new drugs," include energizers and tranquilizers. They are not cures. They can be dangerous. They must be taken carefully and only under the supervision of an expert. They can be very useful in relieving symptoms and in improving the climate for psychotherapy. They have been a special boon in removing the need for E.C.T. in people whose condition would formerly have required the more stringent treatment with E.C.T.

Hospitals

I consider hospitalization a radical form of treatment which must be used with the greatest care. If at all possible, it is best that the patient be treated outside of a hospital and in a normal setting. If he can go on functioning in a regular capacity, so much the better. Hospitalization can be addicting and incapacitating. People unfortunately "learn to use the hospital" as an escape from reality and from the vicissitudes of everyday life. Hospitalization should only be instituted when an expert consultant feels that it is absolutely necessary. Of course, there are conditions in which hospitalization is absolutely required. But remember, hospitals help but don't cure. Psychotherapy following hospitalization is always required. Now, what about choosing a hospital? When this happens, the hospital must be chosen with great care. Are there criteria for a good hospital? Yes! Here they are. These are twelve of them.

1. The physical plant—Emotionally sick people need at least the minimum *comfort* that healthy people do. This includes proper heat, ventilation, beds, linens, clothes, cleanliness, cheerful surroundings, adequate space, grounds to walk on, entertainment facilities, good food, etc. Contrary to misinformed opinion, sick people are not oblivious to physical environment.
2. A hospital director who has the highest professional

qualifications and who chooses his staff accordingly.
3. Good doctor-nurse-attendant-psychologist-social worker-occupational therapist to patient ratios. Unfortunately, there still are huge state institutions with ratios as bad as one doctor per five hundred patients.
4. Adequate staffing so that patients, however sick, regressed or out of control, are seen by a doctor at least once a day and whenever necessary.
5. Hospitals run on a nonprofit basis are usually safer. This is especially true of those that have medical school or university affiliations and teaching programs. There are some good profit-making hospitals, but do make sure that the one of your choice is licensed by the state in which it is located.
6. A hospital in which some form of psychotherapy and occupational therapy take place for every patient, regardless of his or her condition. This hospital never functions in a purely custodial capacity.
7. A hospital which does not ever use physical restraints, straitjackets, manacles, etc., and in which a patient is never physically subdued.
8. A hospital where socializing (visits when appropriate) and a permissive nonclinical, warm, friendly atmosphere prevails.
9. A hospital in which gratuities and bribing play absolutely no role.
10. A hospital which is interested and geared to the possibility of the patient returning to a nonhospital active existence. This can be evidenced in several ways. In this hospital, patients will be kept as active and productive as possible. They will not be permitted to vegetate. Home visits on an increasingly frequent basis will be encouraged as much as possible.
11. A hospital which encourages psychotherapy on discharge and orients the patient accordingly.

12. A hospital in which the personnel at all times respect the dignity, individuality, preferences and needs of each patient as they would any non-patient.

Go over the above criteria before you permit anyone to be hospitalized, but do something else as well. While you may not be a trained psychiatrist, you are entitled to a talk with the man in charge as well as with a nurse, an attendant, and your relative's doctor. Do that! Have a talk and trust your feelings. Do you like these people? Do they feel like interested, good human beings? If they feel right to you and if the hospital pretty well measures up to our list, then our patient is probably in good hands. May I suggest, however, that you reevaluate every few months and that you visit and demonstrate your interest frequently. Interest and concern for the patient are contagious and constructive!

The initial consultation

This initial contact is all important. The psychiatrist will determine the extent and depth of the problems, the sickness—health ratio, the assets and limitations, the prognosis and goals and above all, how to get to those goals. He knows that every patient is not for every psychiatrist. It will be his job to choose the most appropriate therapist (personality-wise) in order to have the most constructive therapeutic relationship possible. One or several interviews may be necessary, as well as possible diagnostic tests, such as the Rorschach Projective Test, figure drawing test, Thematic Apperception test, etc. For these tests, the psychiatrist will make use of the skills of

The Winner's Notebook

an expert in this area, namely a highly trained clinical psychologist.

It is my opinion that the best consultation is with the most highly trained and experienced men. I feel that this criterion applies to psychiatrists trained and certified by psychoanalytic institutes recognized by either the American Academy of Psychoanalysis or the American Psychoanalytic Association. You can contact either organization for the names of consultants in your area.

If help of a more general nature is required, including financial and familial help, then some of the social service agencies are very helpful. These include the Jewish Family Service and Catholic Charities. For help in locating doctors and clinics, you may consult your particular county medical society and the local branch of the National Mental Health Association.

SECTION VI

The End—and the Beginning

This is the last section. It is short. As a beginning to living your life in a more constructive way, I hope that the book's impact will be long.

Who is a winner?

There is no absolute winner and no absolute loser. But there are relative winners and their capacity to win grows and grows. These are some general criteria.

They are people who are happy with who they are, at least sometimes.

They like to be alone and they like to be with other people.

They listen to other people and they decide for themselves.

They are capable of self-assertion rather than having a need for compliance, rebellion, or running away.

They enjoy sex, food, entertainment, work—without guilt and without making a claim on others for fulfillment.

They enjoy today and look forward to tomorrow.

They are capable of spontaneous feelings.

They can give and receive love. They can tolerate the anger of others and get angry and they can forgive and forget.

They know who they are—in limits, in assets, in values, in likes and dislikes, and they are capable of enjoying individuality.

They can invest emotion and enthusiasm in people, causes and things.

They know the difference between real self-fulfillment and fleeting glory.

They care about this world and they appreciate their role and responsibility as part of it.

How?

Ownership of assets; clarifying muddles; knowing the enemy; knowing yourself and how to make it with Max; knowing where and how and who to get help from, if necessary—are formidable allies in becoming a winner. Practice and application are necessary. There are bumps in the road. But the road winds on to wonderful goals. You have an opportunity to be responsible for your own life, in achieving self-fulfillment and in becoming a happier person as a winner.

Index